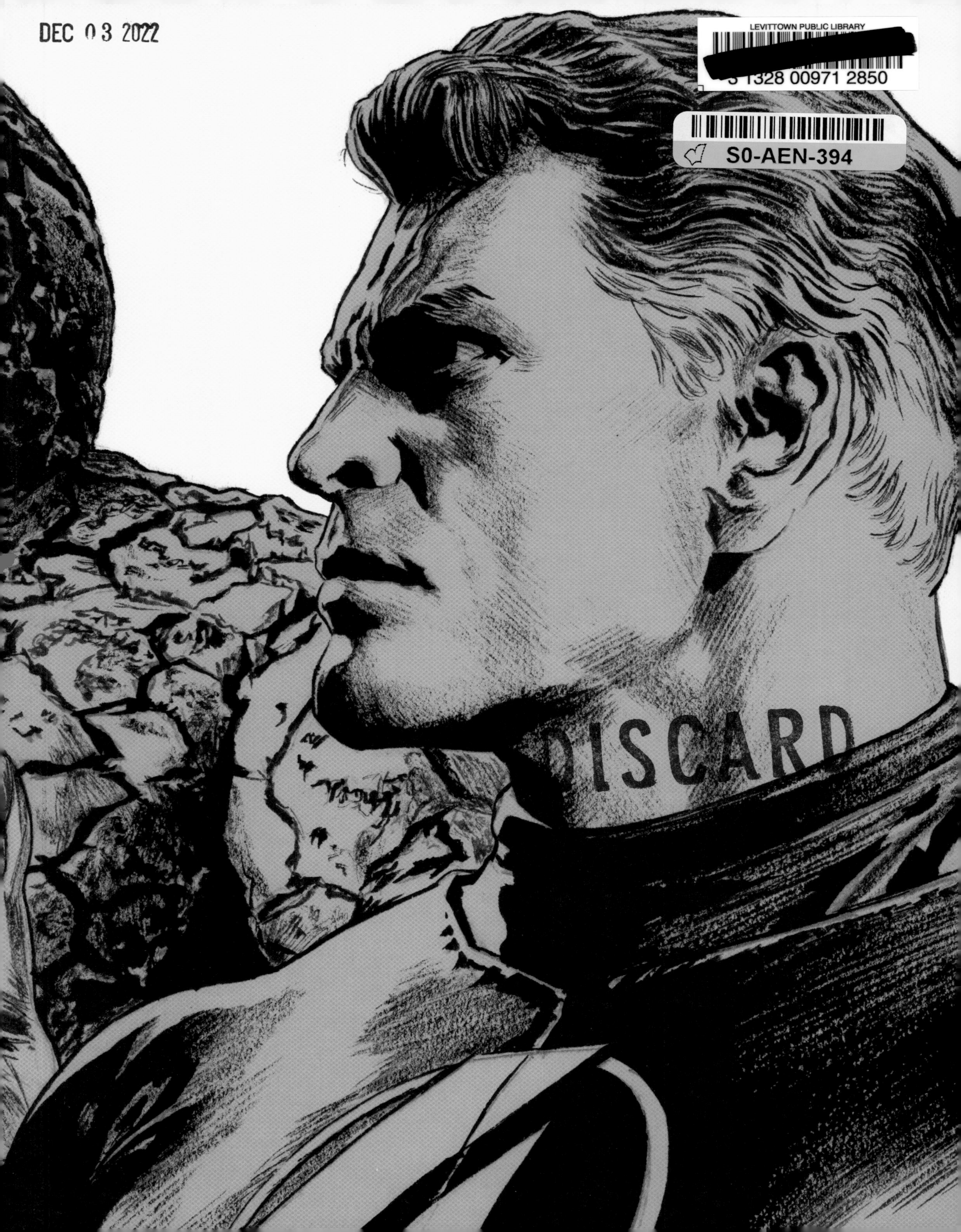

Fantastic Four
Full Circle

by alex ross

Abrams ComicArts • New York

FANTASTIC FOUR

created by
Stan Lee
and **Jack Kirby**

Art and script by
Alex Ross

Colors by
Alex Ross
with **Josh Johnson**

Lettering by
Ariana Maher

For Marvel:
Assistant Editor: Martin Biro
Associate Editor: Annalise Bissa
Editor: Tom Brevoort
Editor in Chief: C. B. Cebulski

For Abrams:
Editor: Charles Kochman
Assistant Editor: Jessica Gotz
Designer: Josh Johnson
Art Director: Pamela Notarantonio
Managing Editor: Marie Oishi
Production Manager: Alison Gervais

Library of Congress Cataloging Number 2021946490

ISBN 978-1-4197-6167-6
eISBN 978-1-64700-781-2

MARVEL © 2022 MARVEL

Original files prepared by Josh Johnson

Published in 2022 by Abrams ComicArts®, an imprint of ABRAMS.
All rights reserved. No portion of this book may be reproduced,
stored in a retrieval system, or transmitteed in any form or by
any means, mechanical, electronic, photocopying, recording,
or otherwise, without written permission from the publisher.

Printed and bound in China
10 9 8 7 6 5 4 3 2

Abrams ComicArts books are available at special discounts when
purchased in quantity for premiums and promotions as well as
fundraising or educational use. Special editions can also be created
to specification. For details, contact specialsales@abramsbooks.com
or the address below.

Abrams ComicArts® is a registered trademark of Harry N. Abrams, Inc.

ABRAMS The Art of Books
195 Broadway, New York, NY 10007
abramsbooks.com

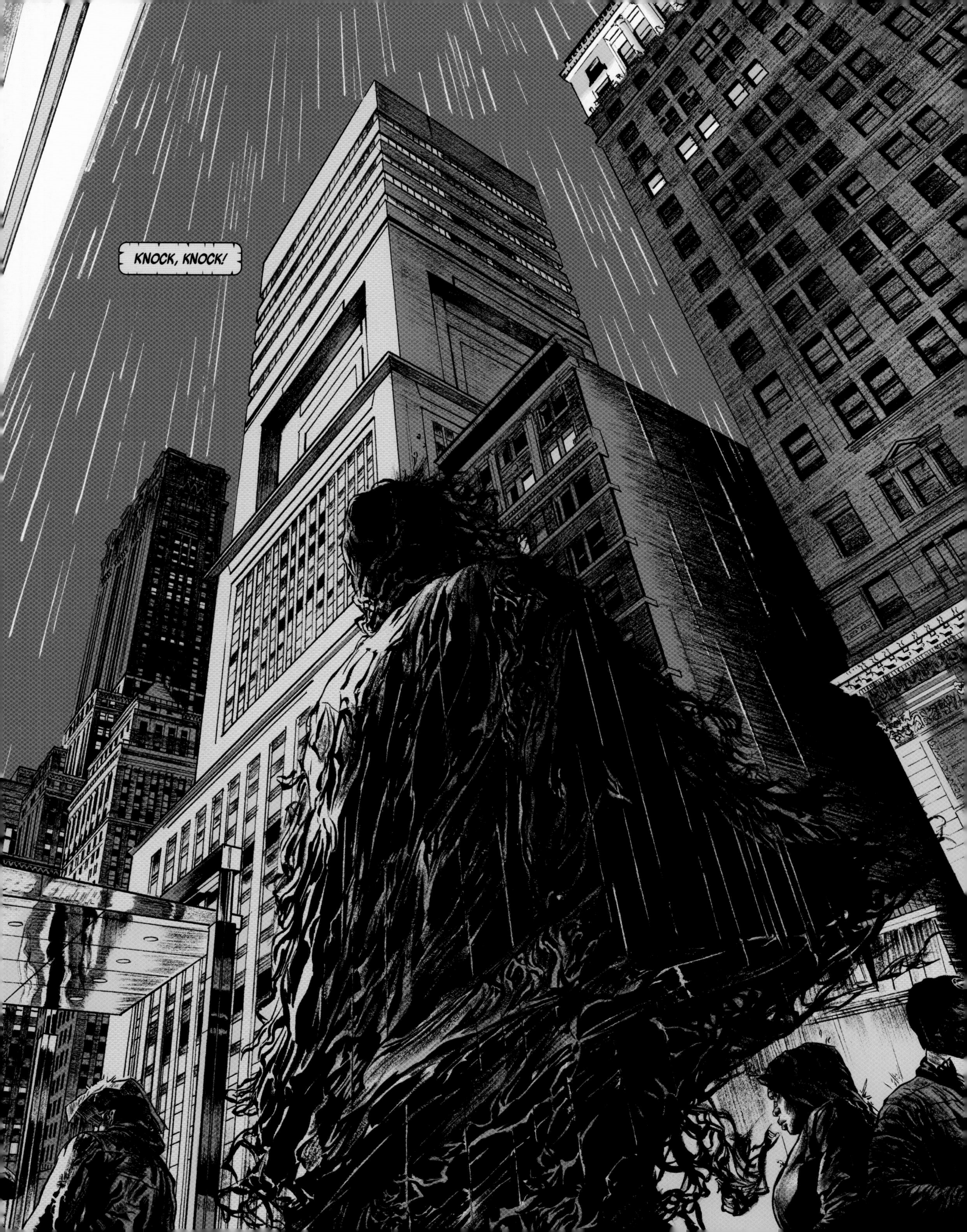
KNOCK, KNOCK!

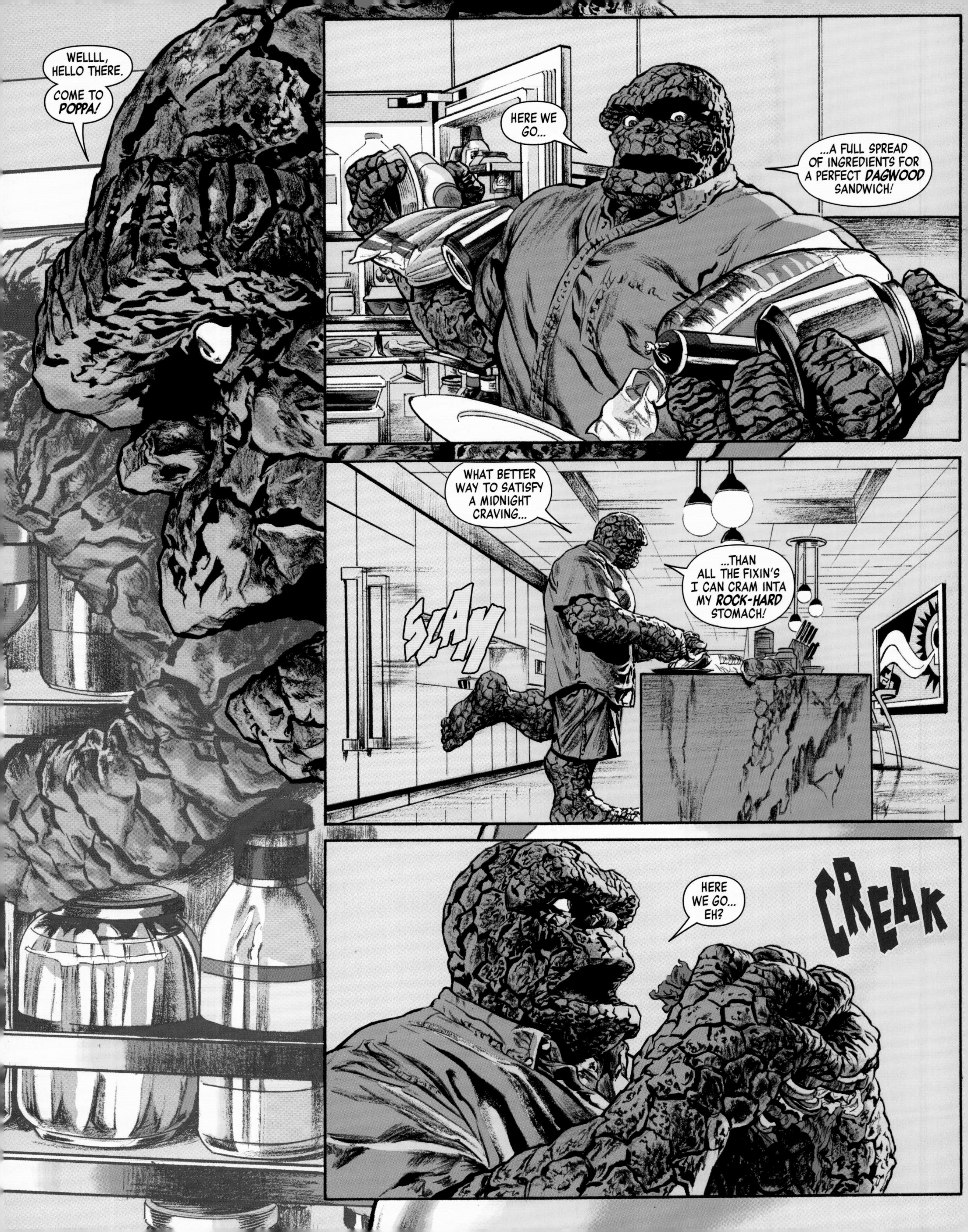
WELLLL, HELLO THERE.
COME TO POPPA!
HERE WE GO...
...A FULL SPREAD OF INGREDIENTS FOR A PERFECT DAGWOOD SANDWICH!
WHAT BETTER WAY TO SATISFY A MIDNIGHT CRAVING...
SLAM
...THAN ALL THE FIXIN'S I CAN CRAM INTA MY ROCK-HARD STOMACH!
HERE WE GO... EH?
CREAK

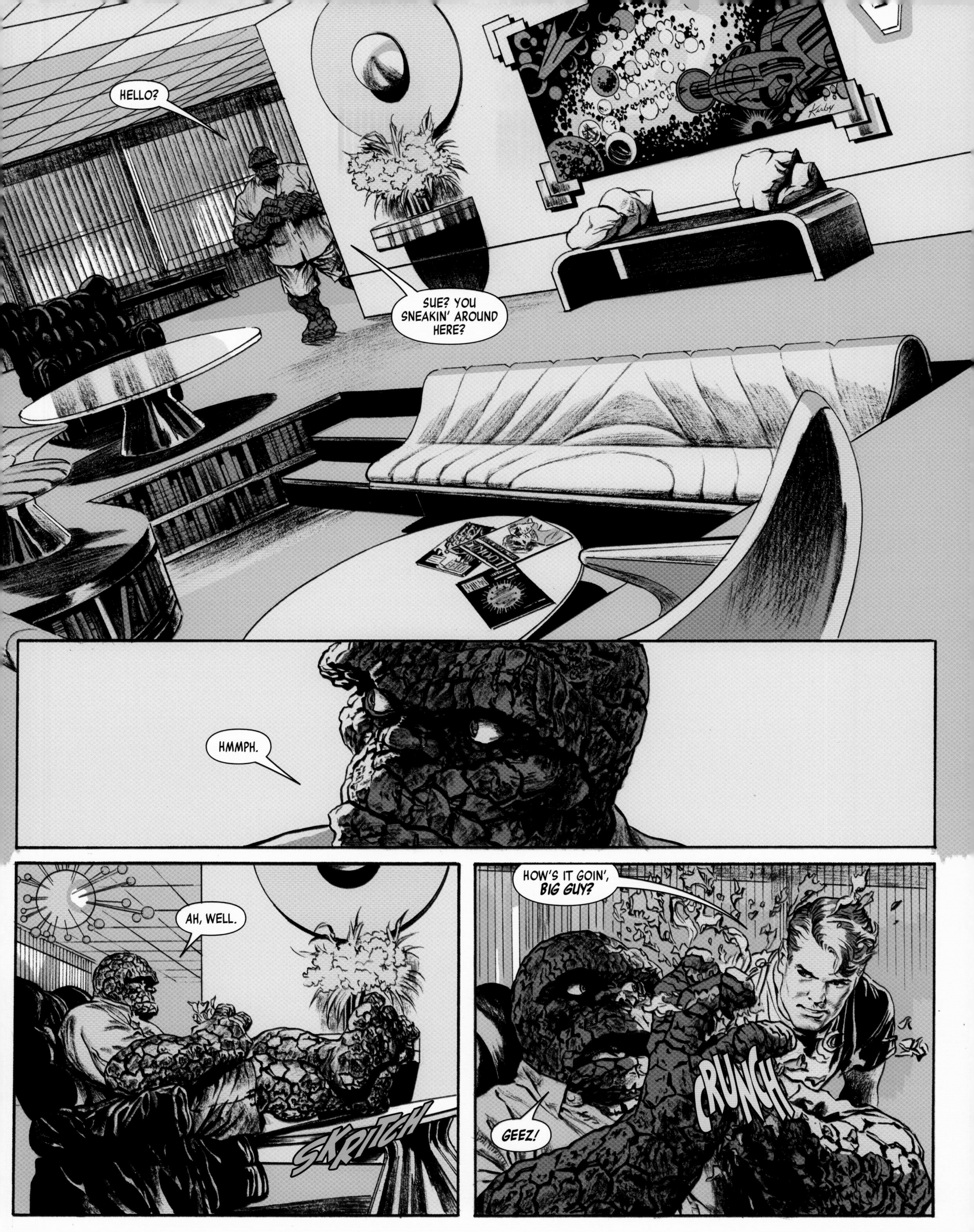
HELLO?
SUE? YOU SNEAKIN' AROUND HERE?
HMMPH.
AH, WELL.
SKRITCH
HOW'S IT GOIN', BIG GUY?
CRUNCH
GEEZ!

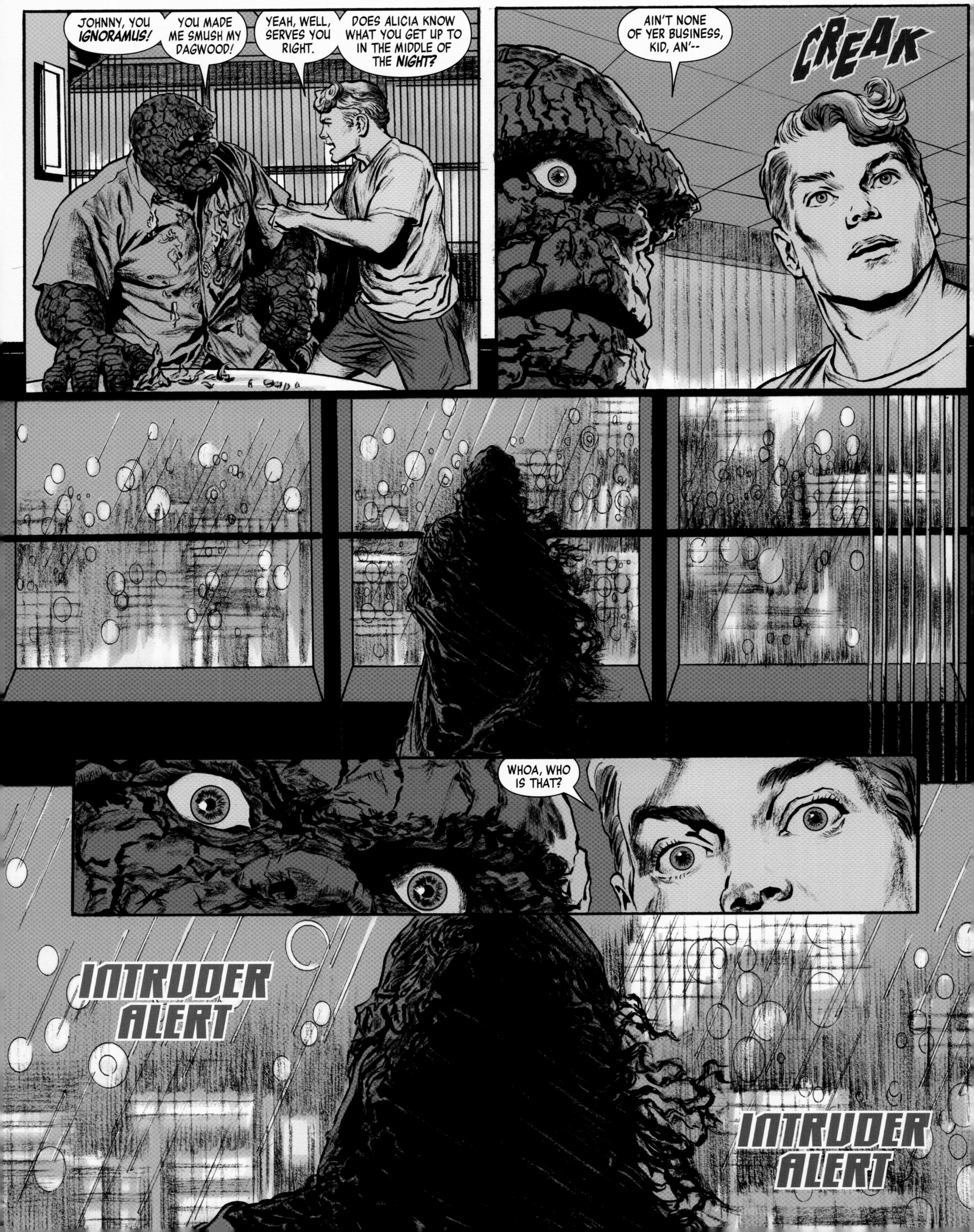
JOHNNY, YOU IGNORAMUS!
YOU MADE ME SMUSH MY DAGWOOD!
YEAH, WELL, SERVES YOU RIGHT.
DOES ALICIA KNOW WHAT YOU GET UP TO IN THE MIDDLE OF THE NIGHT?
AIN'T NONE OF YER BUSINESS, KID, AN'--
CREAK
WHOA, WHO IS THAT?
INTRUDER ALERT
INTRUDER ALERT

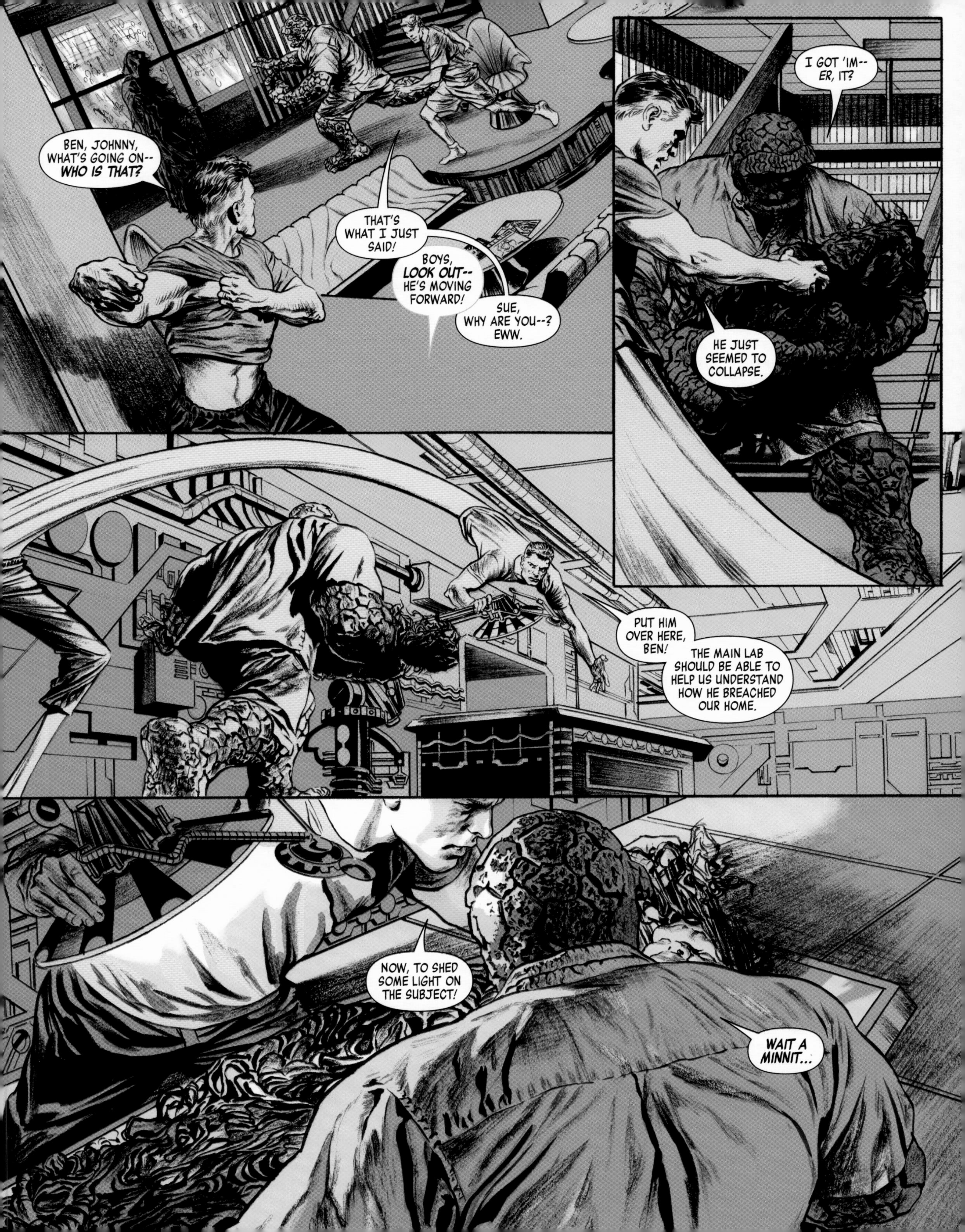
BEN, JOHNNY, WHAT'S GOING ON-- **WHO IS THAT?**
THAT'S WHAT I JUST SAID!
BOYS, **LOOK OUT--** HE'S MOVING FORWARD!
SUE, WHY ARE YOU--? EWW.
I GOT 'IM-- ER, IT?
HE JUST SEEMED TO COLLAPSE.
PUT HIM OVER HERE, BEN!
THE MAIN LAB SHOULD BE ABLE TO HELP US UNDERSTAND HOW HE BREACHED OUR HOME.
NOW, TO SHED SOME LIGHT ON THE SUBJECT!
WAIT A MINNIT...

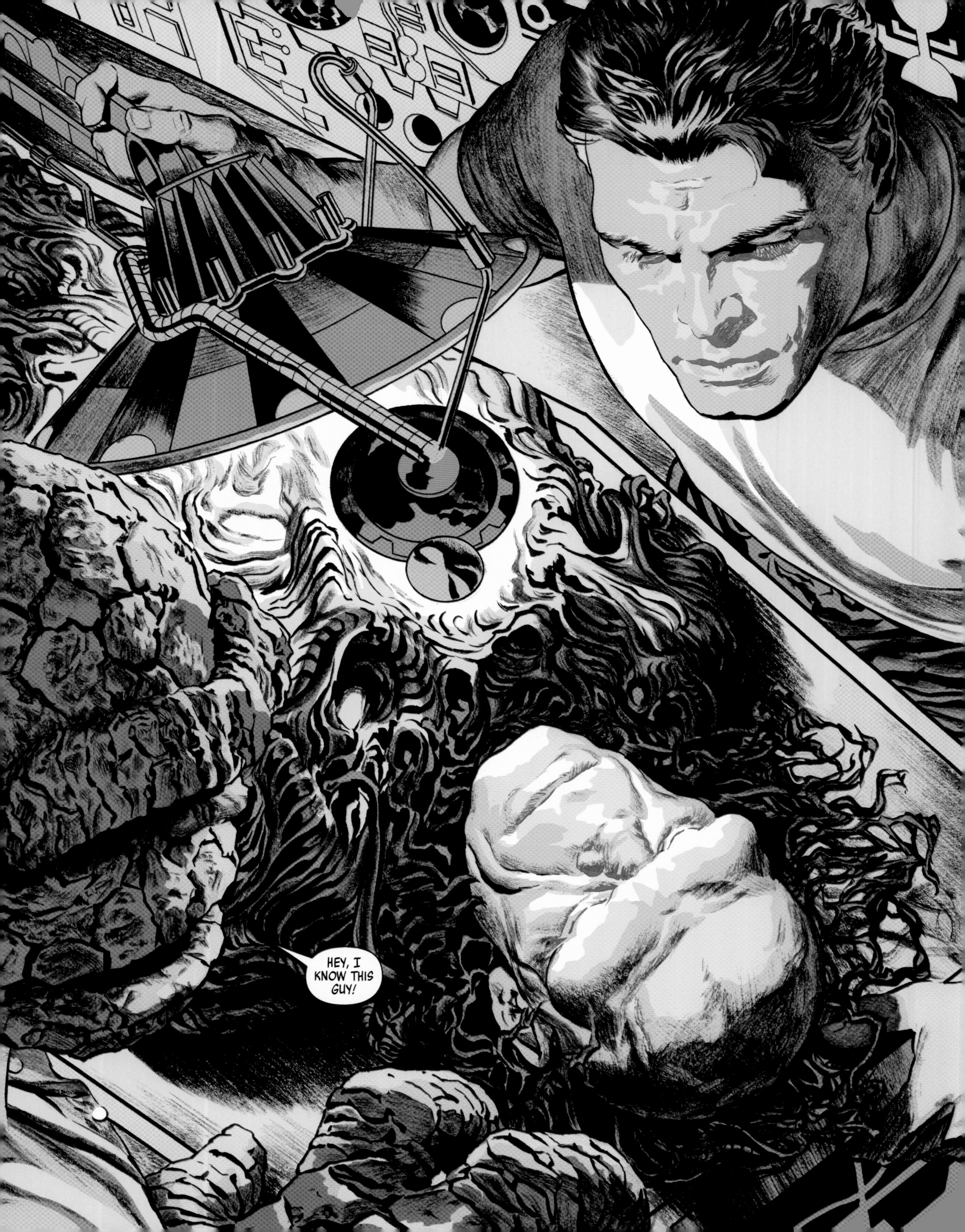
HEY, I KNOW THIS GUY!

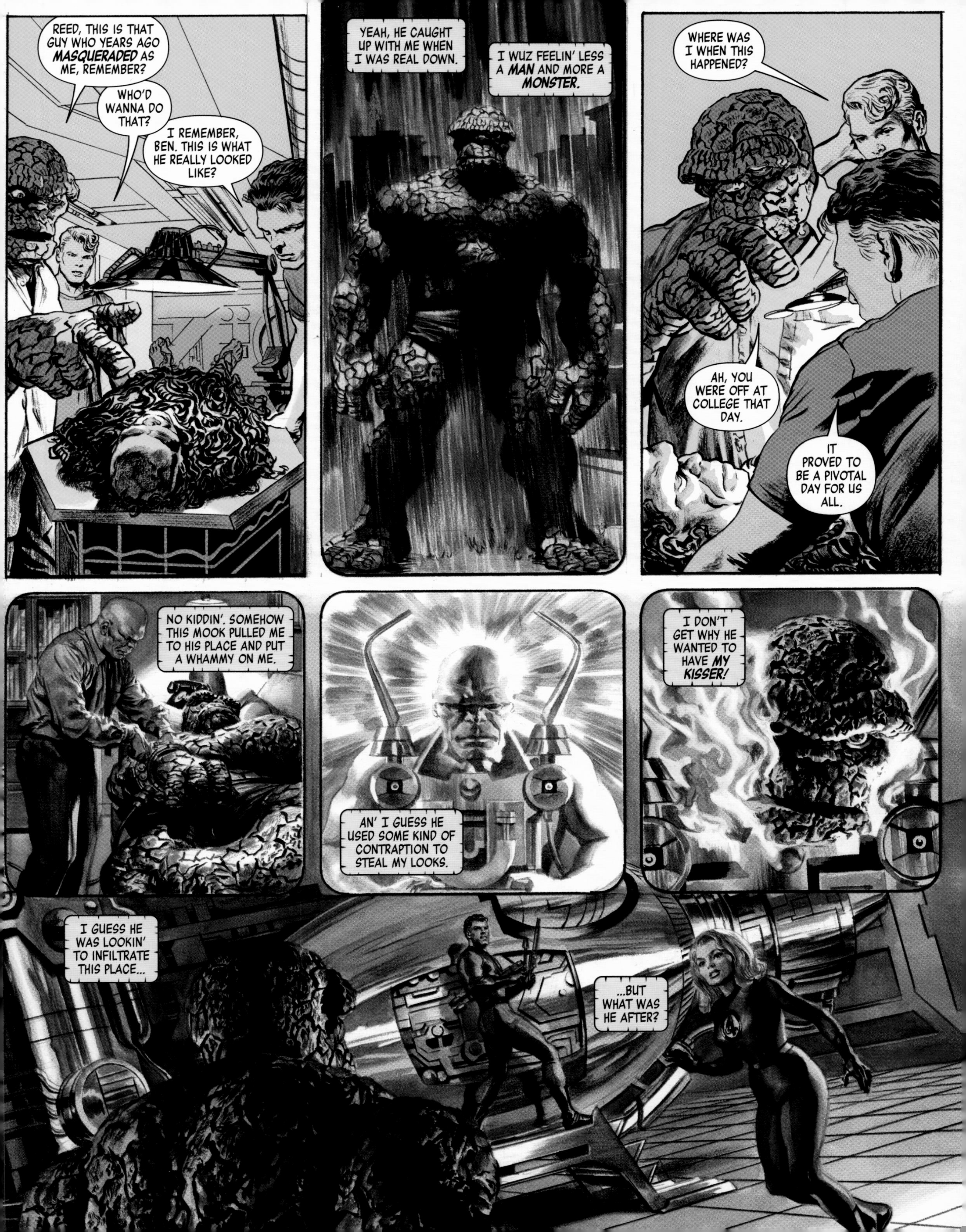
REED, THIS IS THAT GUY WHO YEARS AGO MASQUERADED AS ME, REMEMBER?
WHO'D WANNA DO THAT?
I REMEMBER, BEN. THIS IS WHAT HE REALLY LOOKED LIKE?
YEAH, HE CAUGHT UP WITH ME WHEN I WAS REAL DOWN.
I WUZ FEELIN' LESS A MAN AND MORE A MONSTER.
WHERE WAS I WHEN THIS HAPPENED?
AH, YOU WERE OFF AT COLLEGE THAT DAY.
IT PROVED TO BE A PIVOTAL DAY FOR US ALL.
NO KIDDIN'. SOMEHOW THIS MOOK PULLED ME TO HIS PLACE AND PUT A WHAMMY ON ME.
AN' I GUESS HE USED SOME KIND OF CONTRAPTION TO STEAL MY LOOKS.
I DON'T GET WHY HE WANTED TO HAVE MY KISSER!
I GUESS HE WAS LOOKIN' TO INFILTRATE THIS PLACE...
...BUT WHAT WAS HE AFTER?

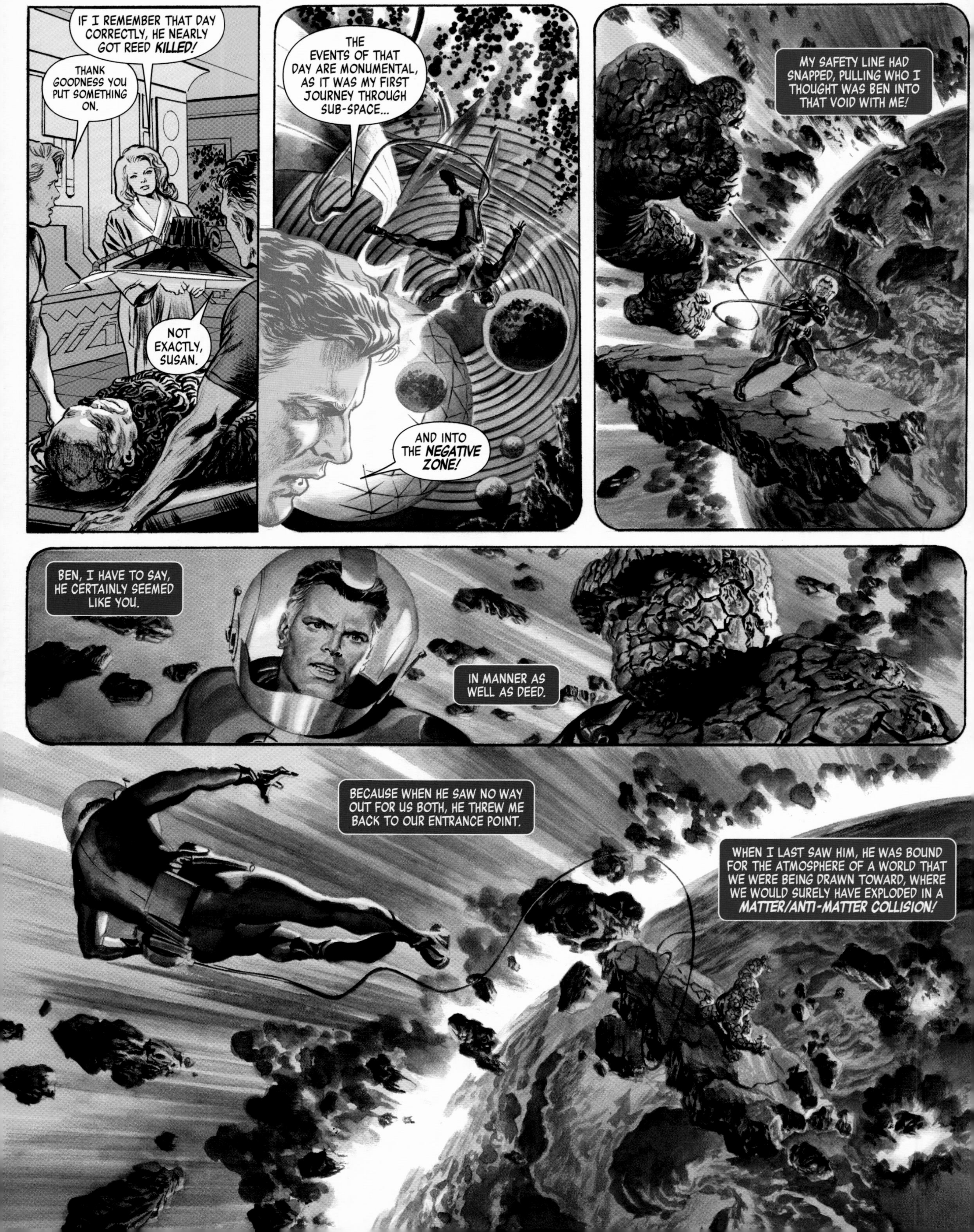
IF I REMEMBER THAT DAY CORRECTLY, HE NEARLY GOT REED **KILLED!**
THANK GOODNESS YOU PUT SOMETHING ON.
NOT EXACTLY, SUSAN.
THE EVENTS OF THAT DAY ARE MONUMENTAL, AS IT WAS MY FIRST JOURNEY THROUGH SUB-SPACE...
AND INTO THE **NEGATIVE ZONE!**
MY SAFETY LINE HAD SNAPPED, PULLING WHO I THOUGHT WAS BEN INTO THAT VOID WITH ME!
BEN, I HAVE TO SAY, HE CERTAINLY SEEMED LIKE YOU.
IN MANNER AS WELL AS DEED.
BECAUSE WHEN HE SAW NO WAY OUT FOR US BOTH, HE THREW ME BACK TO OUR ENTRANCE POINT.
WHEN I LAST SAW HIM, HE WAS BOUND FOR THE ATMOSPHERE OF A WORLD THAT WE WERE BEING DRAWN TOWARD, WHERE WE WOULD SURELY HAVE EXPLODED IN A ***MATTER/ANTI-MATTER COLLISION!***

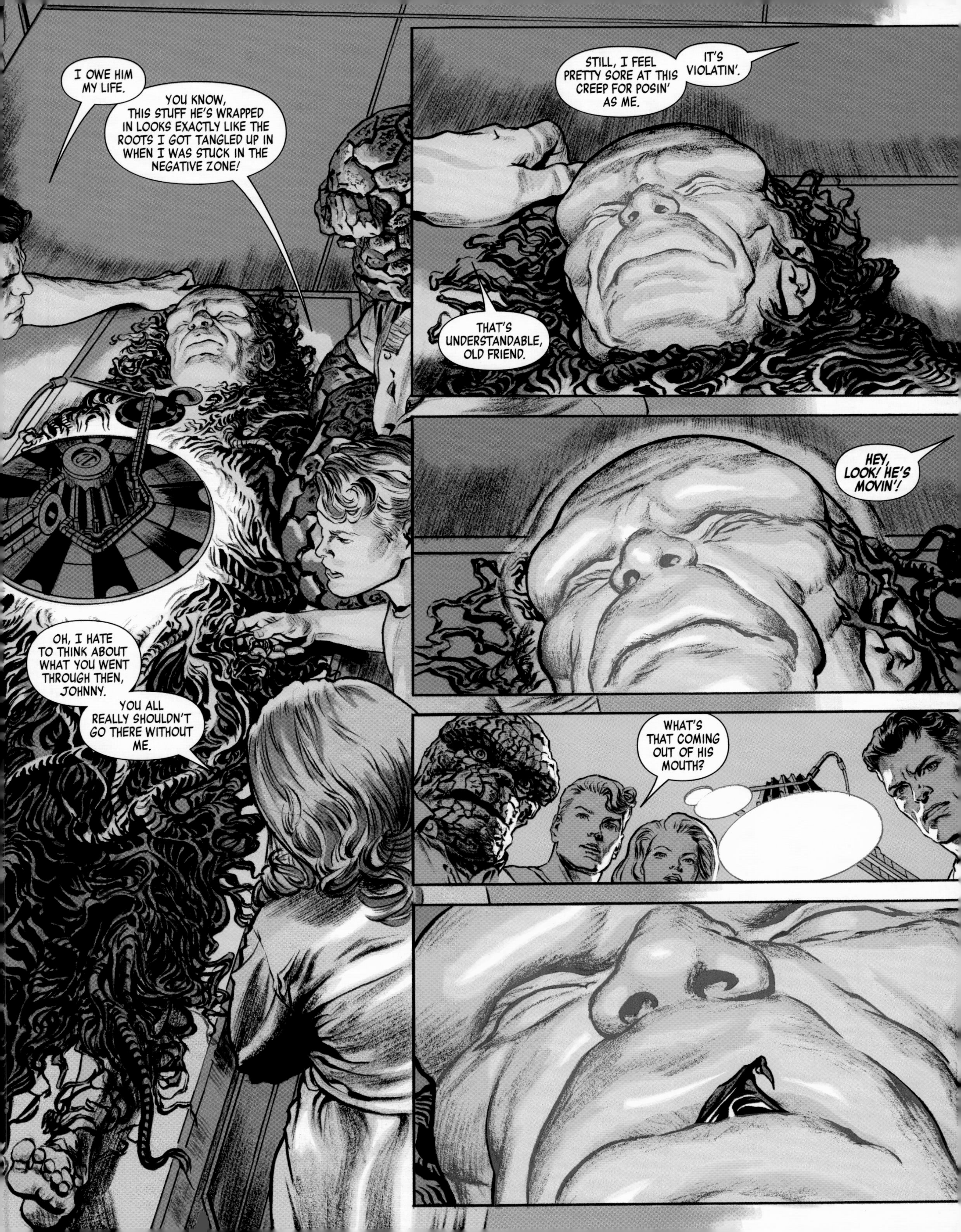
I OWE HIM MY LIFE.
YOU KNOW, THIS STUFF HE'S WRAPPED IN LOOKS EXACTLY LIKE THE ROOTS I GOT TANGLED UP IN WHEN I WAS STUCK IN THE NEGATIVE ZONE!
OH, I HATE TO THINK ABOUT WHAT YOU WENT THROUGH THEN, JOHNNY.
YOU ALL REALLY SHOULDN'T GO THERE WITHOUT ME.
STILL, I FEEL PRETTY SORE AT THIS CREEP FOR POSIN' AS ME.
IT'S VIOLATIN'.
THAT'S UNDERSTANDABLE, OLD FRIEND.
HEY, LOOK! HE'S MOVIN'!
WHAT'S THAT COMING OUT OF HIS MOUTH?

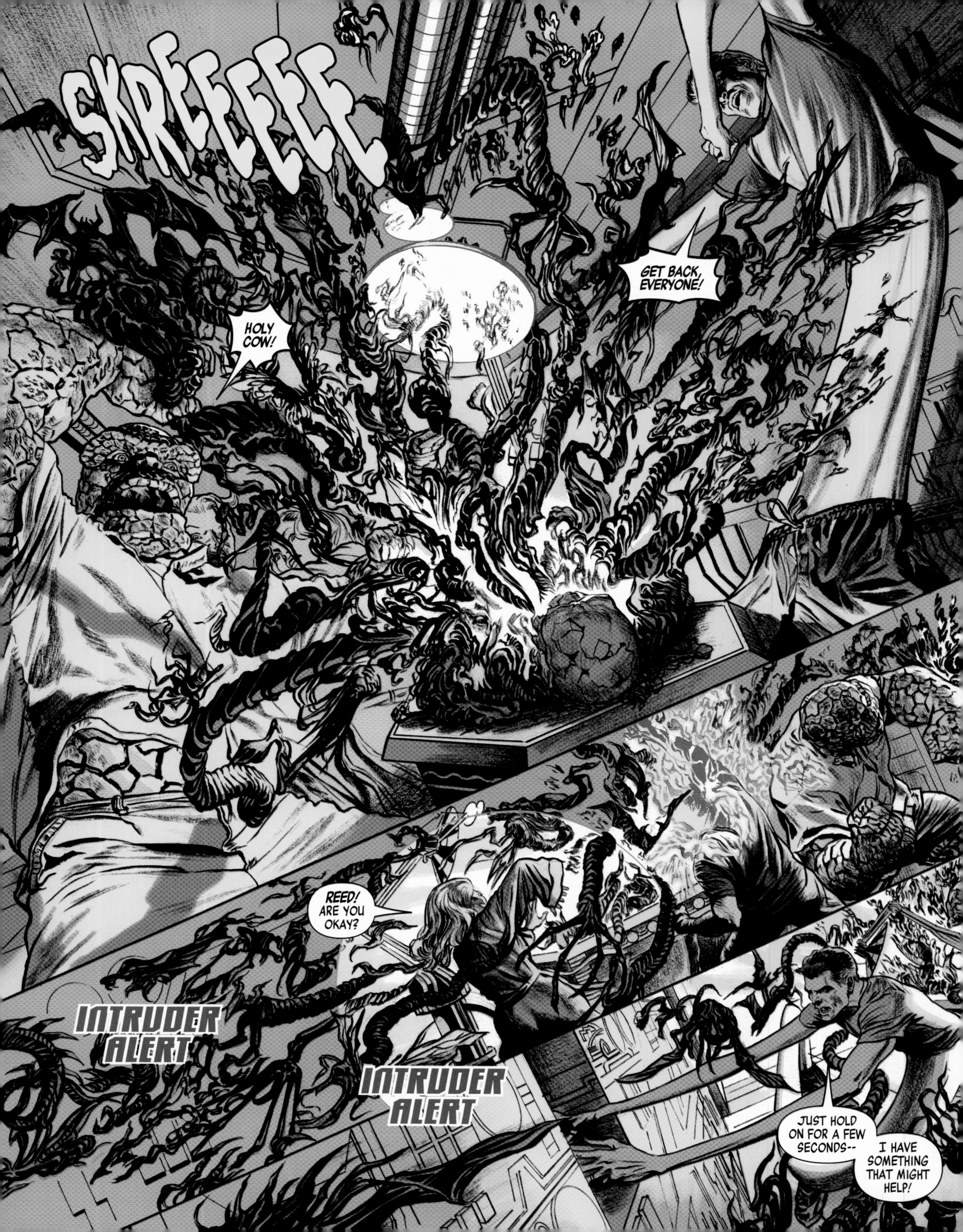
SKREEEEEE
HOLY COW!
GET BACK, EVERYONE!
REED! ARE YOU OKAY?
INTRUDER ALERT
INTRUDER ALERT
JUST HOLD ON FOR A FEW SECONDS--
I HAVE SOMETHING THAT MIGHT HELP!

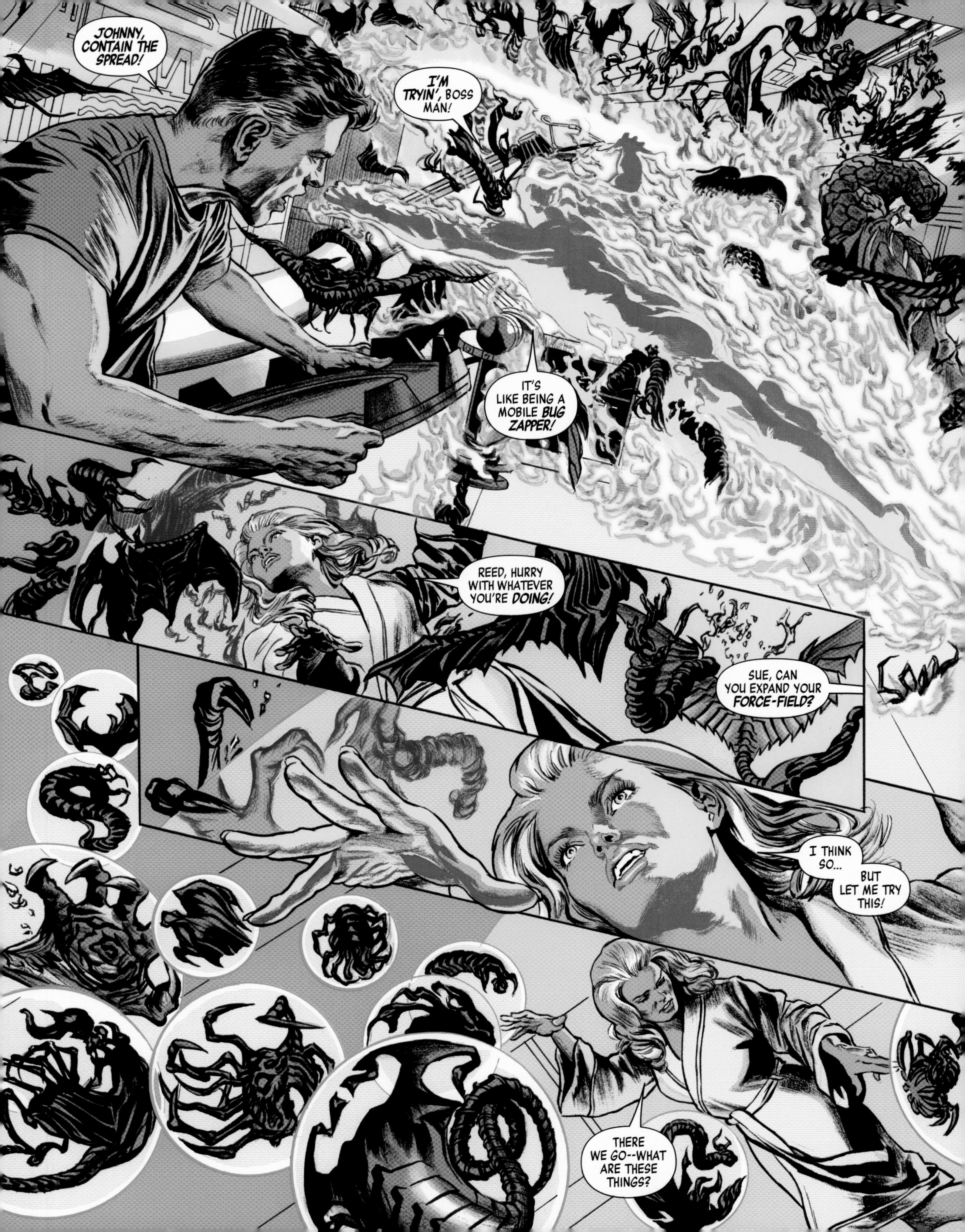
JOHNNY, CONTAIN THE SPREAD!
I'M TRYIN', BOSS MAN!
IT'S LIKE BEING A MOBILE BUG ZAPPER!
REED, HURRY WITH WHATEVER YOU'RE DOING!
SUE, CAN YOU EXPAND YOUR FORCE-FIELD?
I THINK SO...
BUT LET ME TRY THIS!
THERE WE GO--WHAT ARE THESE THINGS?

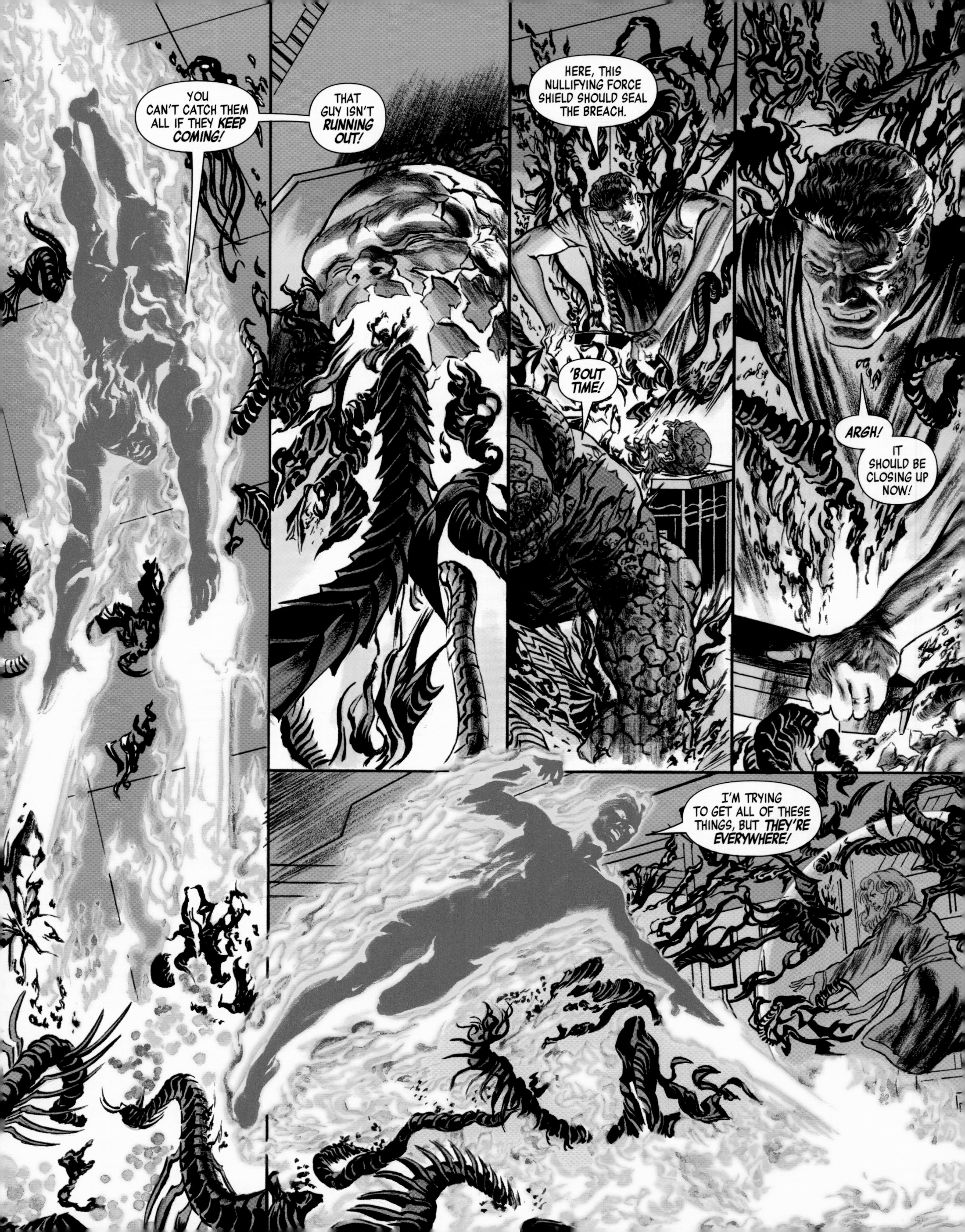
YOU CAN'T CATCH THEM ALL IF THEY KEEP COMING!
THAT GUY ISN'T RUNNING OUT!
HERE, THIS NULLIFYING FORCE SHIELD SHOULD SEAL THE BREACH.
'BOUT TIME!
ARGH!
IT SHOULD BE CLOSING UP NOW!
I'M TRYING TO GET ALL OF THESE THINGS, BUT THEY'RE EVERYWHERE!

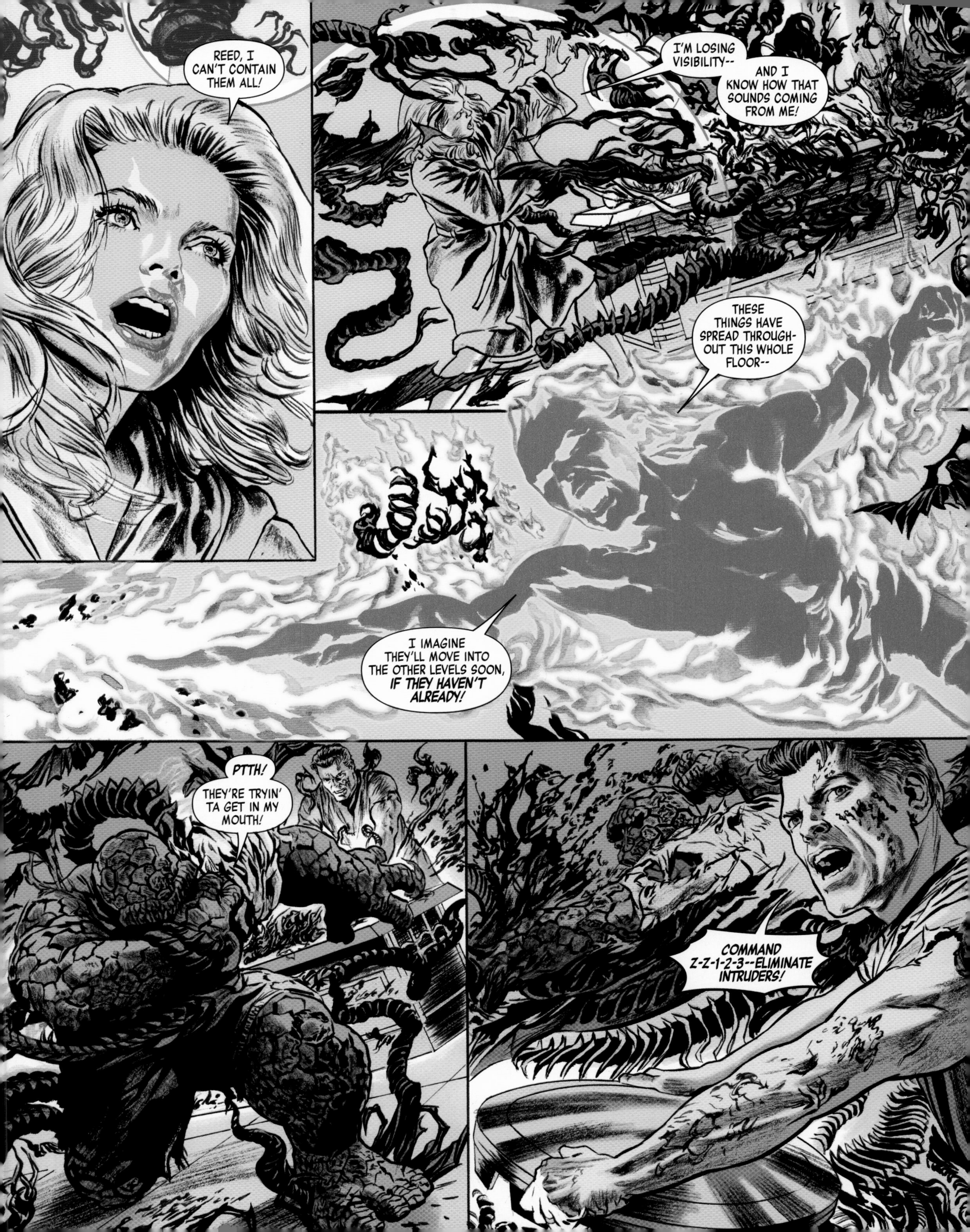
REED, I CAN'T CONTAIN THEM ALL!
I'M LOSING VISIBILITY--
AND I KNOW HOW THAT SOUNDS COMING FROM ME!
THESE THINGS HAVE SPREAD THROUGH-OUT THIS WHOLE FLOOR--
I IMAGINE THEY'LL MOVE INTO THE OTHER LEVELS SOON, IF THEY HAVEN'T ALREADY!
PTTH!
THEY'RE TRYIN' TA GET IN MY MOUTH!
COMMAND Z-Z-1-2-3--ELIMINATE INTRUDERS!

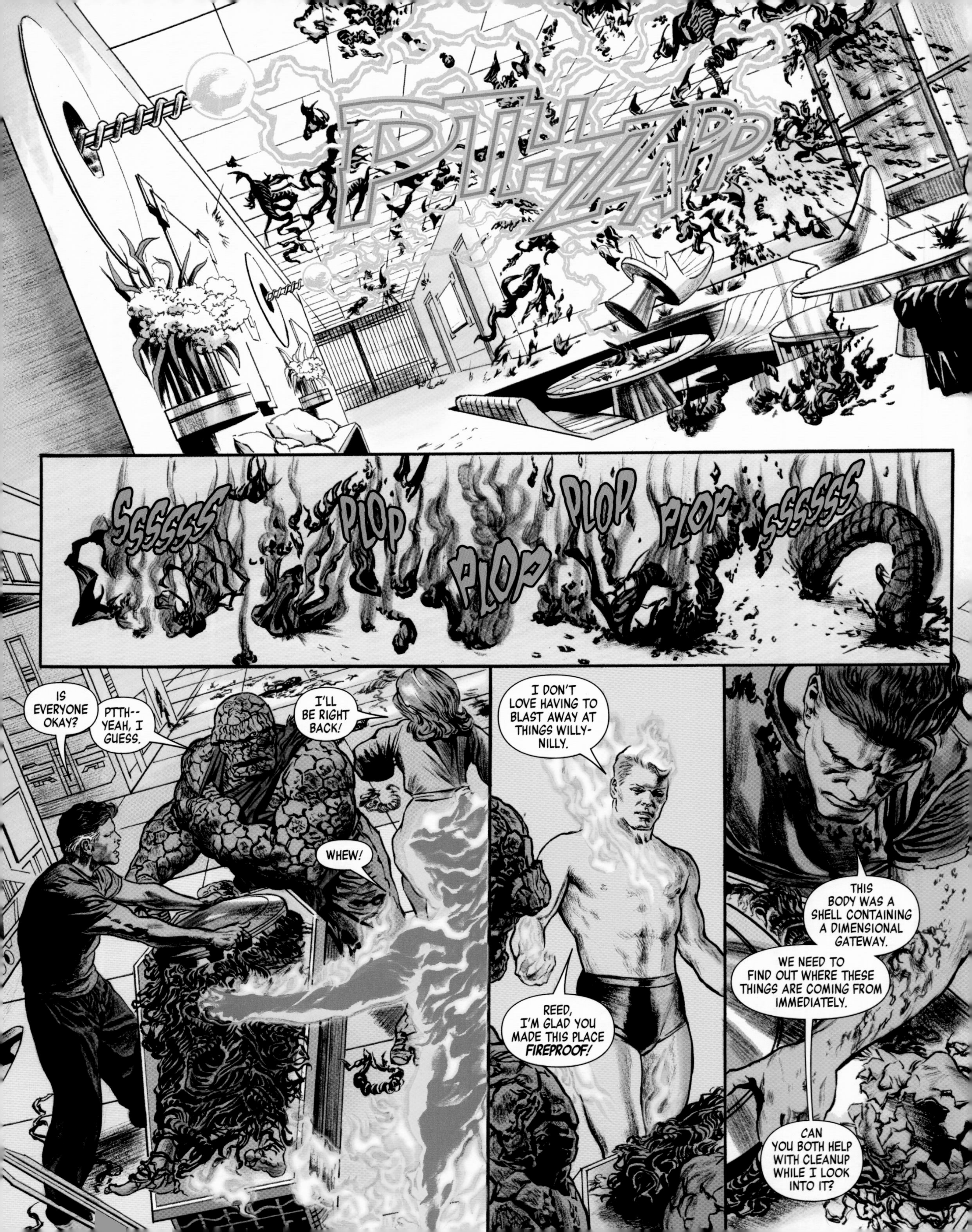
PTTHZZAPP
SSSSSS
PLOP
PLOP
PLOP
PLOP
SSSSSS
IS EVERYONE OKAY?
PTTH-- YEAH, I GUESS.
I'LL BE RIGHT BACK!
WHEW!
I DON'T LOVE HAVING TO BLAST AWAY AT THINGS WILLY-NILLY.
REED, I'M GLAD YOU MADE THIS PLACE FIREPROOF!
THIS BODY WAS A SHELL CONTAINING A DIMENSIONAL GATEWAY.
WE NEED TO FIND OUT WHERE THESE THINGS ARE COMING FROM IMMEDIATELY.
CAN YOU BOTH HELP WITH CLEANUP WHILE I LOOK INTO IT?

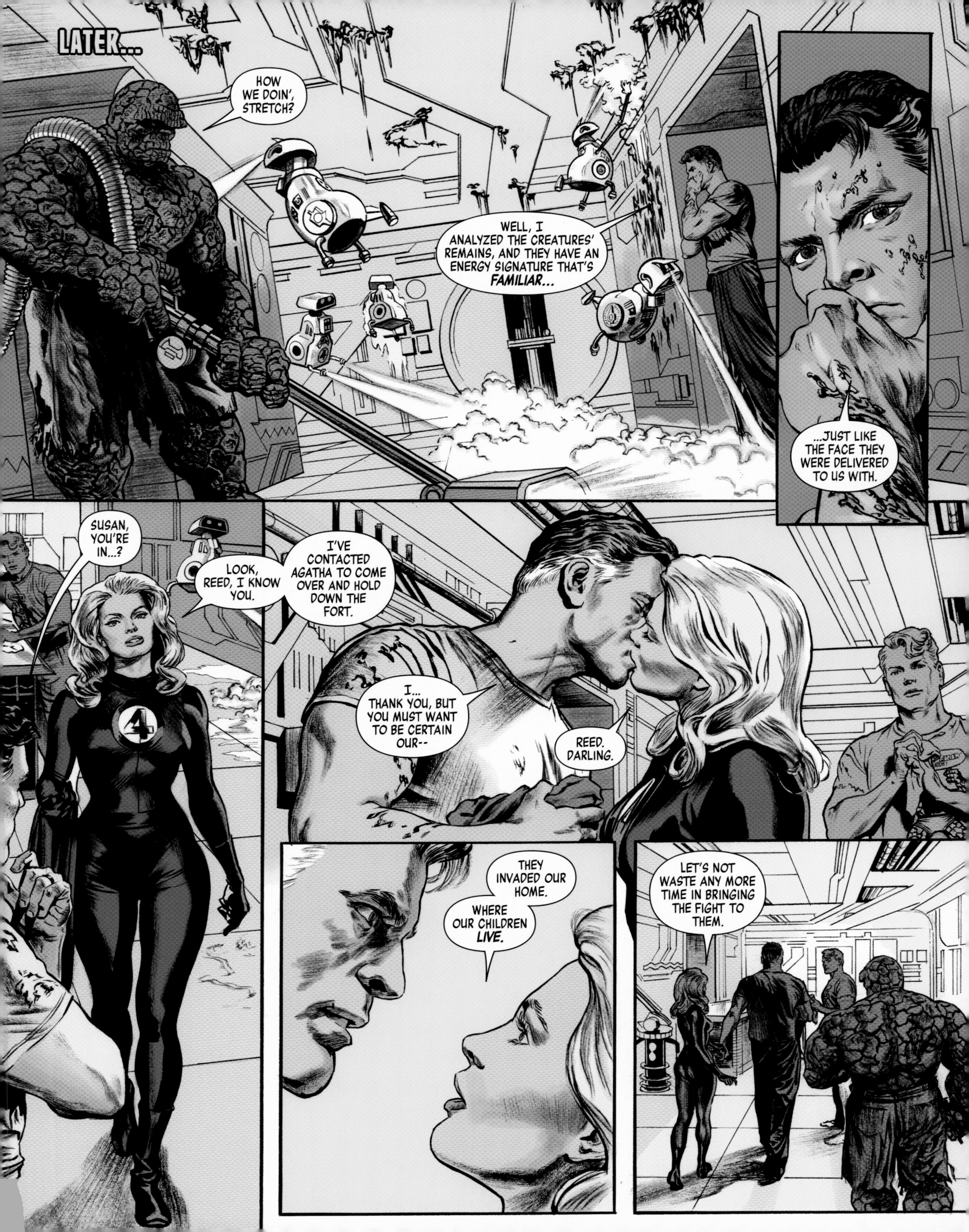
LATER...
HOW WE DOIN', STRETCH?
WELL, I ANALYZED THE CREATURES' REMAINS, AND THEY HAVE AN ENERGY SIGNATURE THAT'S FAMILIAR...
...JUST LIKE THE FACE THEY WERE DELIVERED TO US WITH.
SUSAN, YOU'RE IN...?
LOOK, REED, I KNOW YOU.
I'VE CONTACTED AGATHA TO COME OVER AND HOLD DOWN THE FORT.
I... THANK YOU, BUT YOU MUST WANT TO BE CERTAIN OUR--
REED. DARLING.
THEY INVADED OUR HOME.
WHERE OUR CHILDREN LIVE.
LET'S NOT WASTE ANY MORE TIME IN BRINGING THE FIGHT TO THEM.

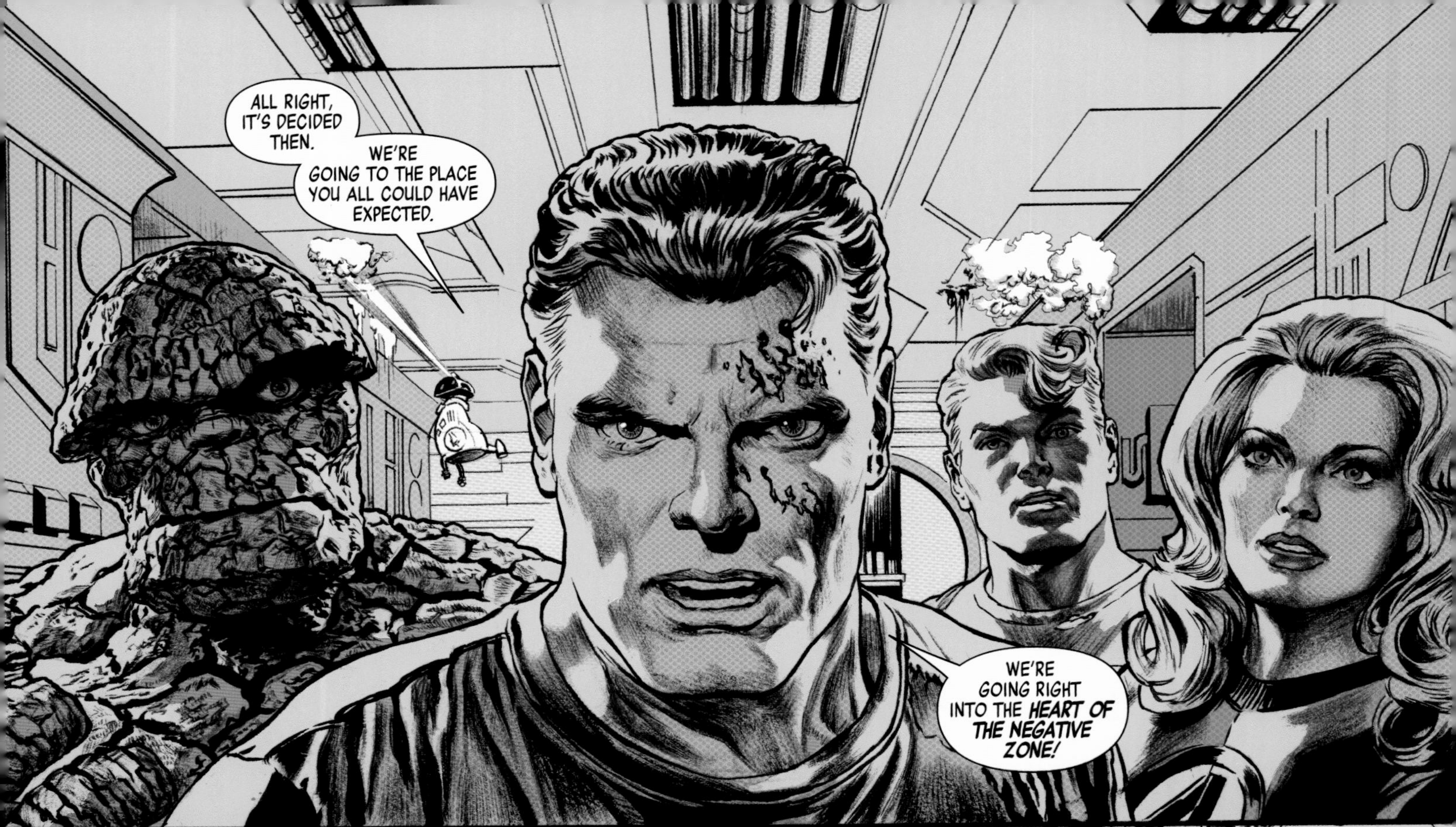
ALL RIGHT, IT'S DECIDED THEN.
WE'RE GOING TO THE PLACE YOU ALL COULD HAVE EXPECTED.
WE'RE GOING RIGHT INTO THE **HEART OF THE NEGATIVE ZONE!**

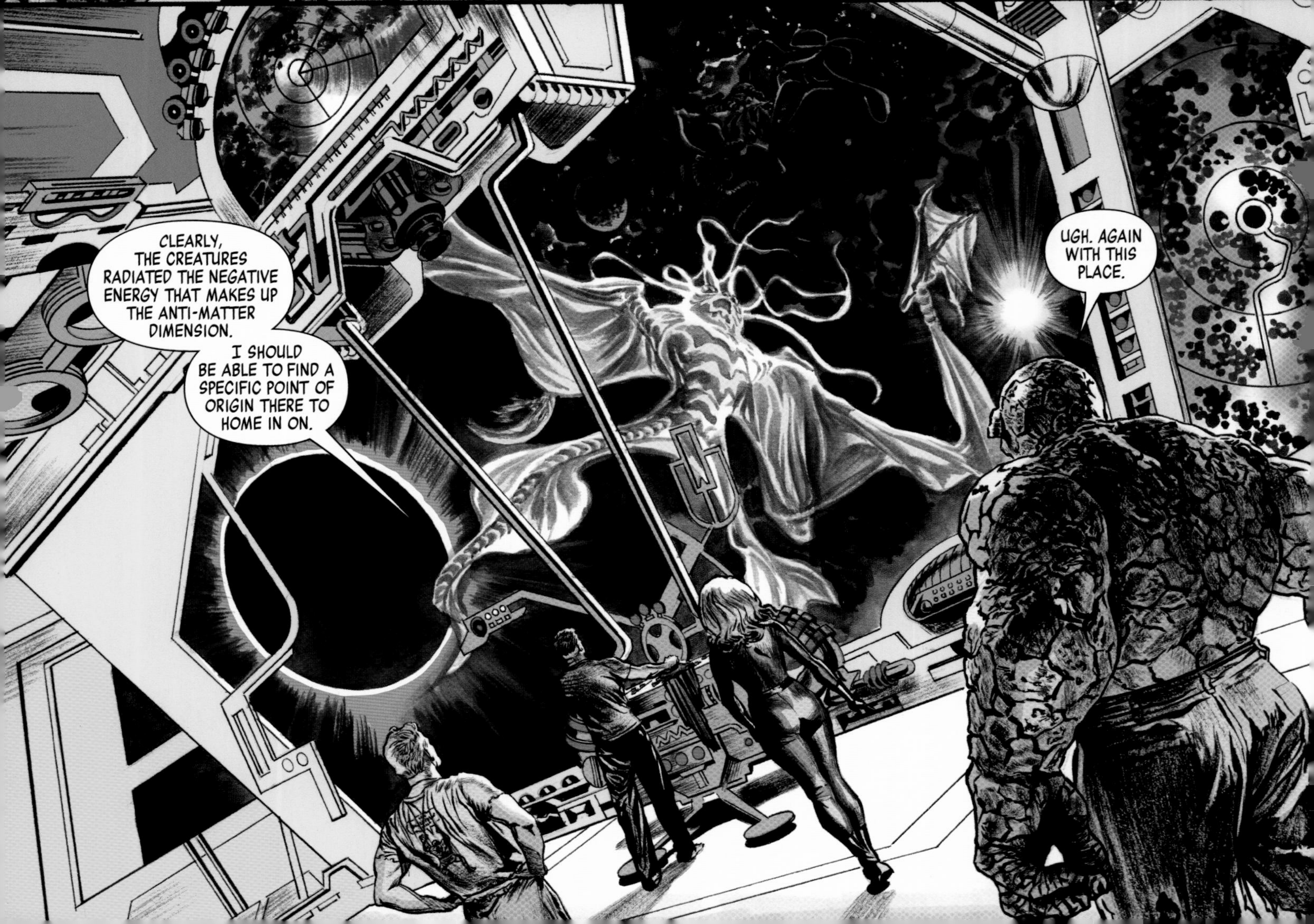
CLEARLY, THE CREATURES RADIATED THE NEGATIVE ENERGY THAT MAKES UP THE ANTI-MATTER DIMENSION.
I SHOULD BE ABLE TO FIND A SPECIFIC POINT OF ORIGIN THERE TO HOME IN ON.
UGH. AGAIN WITH THIS PLACE.

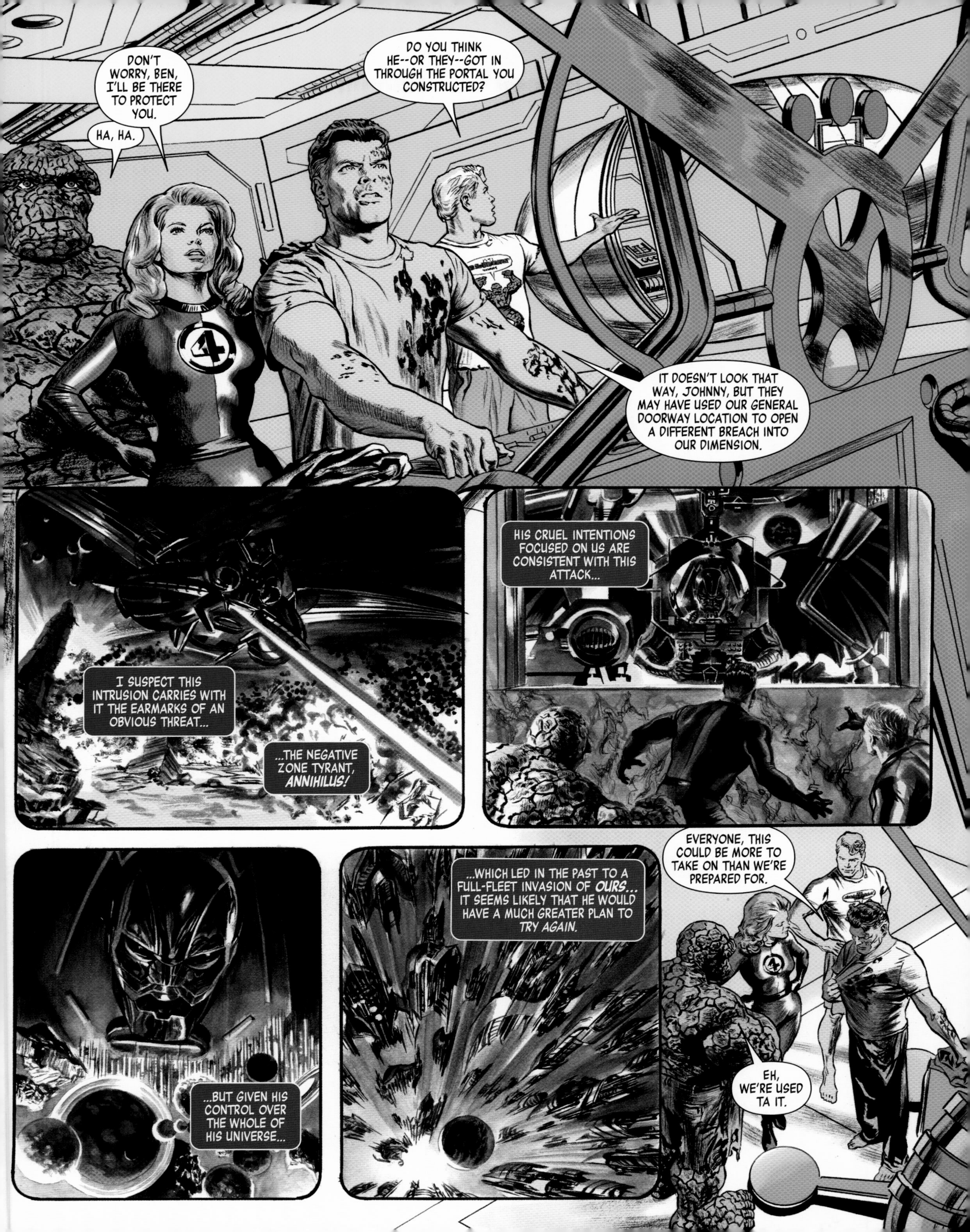

DON'T WORRY, BEN, I'LL BE THERE TO PROTECT YOU.
HA, HA.
DO YOU THINK HE--OR THEY--GOT IN THROUGH THE PORTAL YOU CONSTRUCTED?
IT DOESN'T LOOK THAT WAY, JOHNNY, BUT THEY MAY HAVE USED OUR GENERAL DOORWAY LOCATION TO OPEN A DIFFERENT BREACH INTO OUR DIMENSION.
I SUSPECT THIS INTRUSION CARRIES WITH IT THE EARMARKS OF AN OBVIOUS THREAT...
...THE NEGATIVE ZONE TYRANT, *ANNIHILUS!*
HIS CRUEL INTENTIONS FOCUSED ON US ARE CONSISTENT WITH THIS ATTACK...
...BUT GIVEN HIS CONTROL OVER THE WHOLE OF HIS UNIVERSE...
...WHICH LED IN THE PAST TO A FULL-FLEET INVASION OF ***OURS...*** IT SEEMS LIKELY THAT HE WOULD HAVE A MUCH GREATER PLAN TO *TRY AGAIN.*
EVERYONE, THIS COULD BE MORE TO TAKE ON THAN WE'RE PREPARED FOR.
EH, WE'RE USED TA IT.

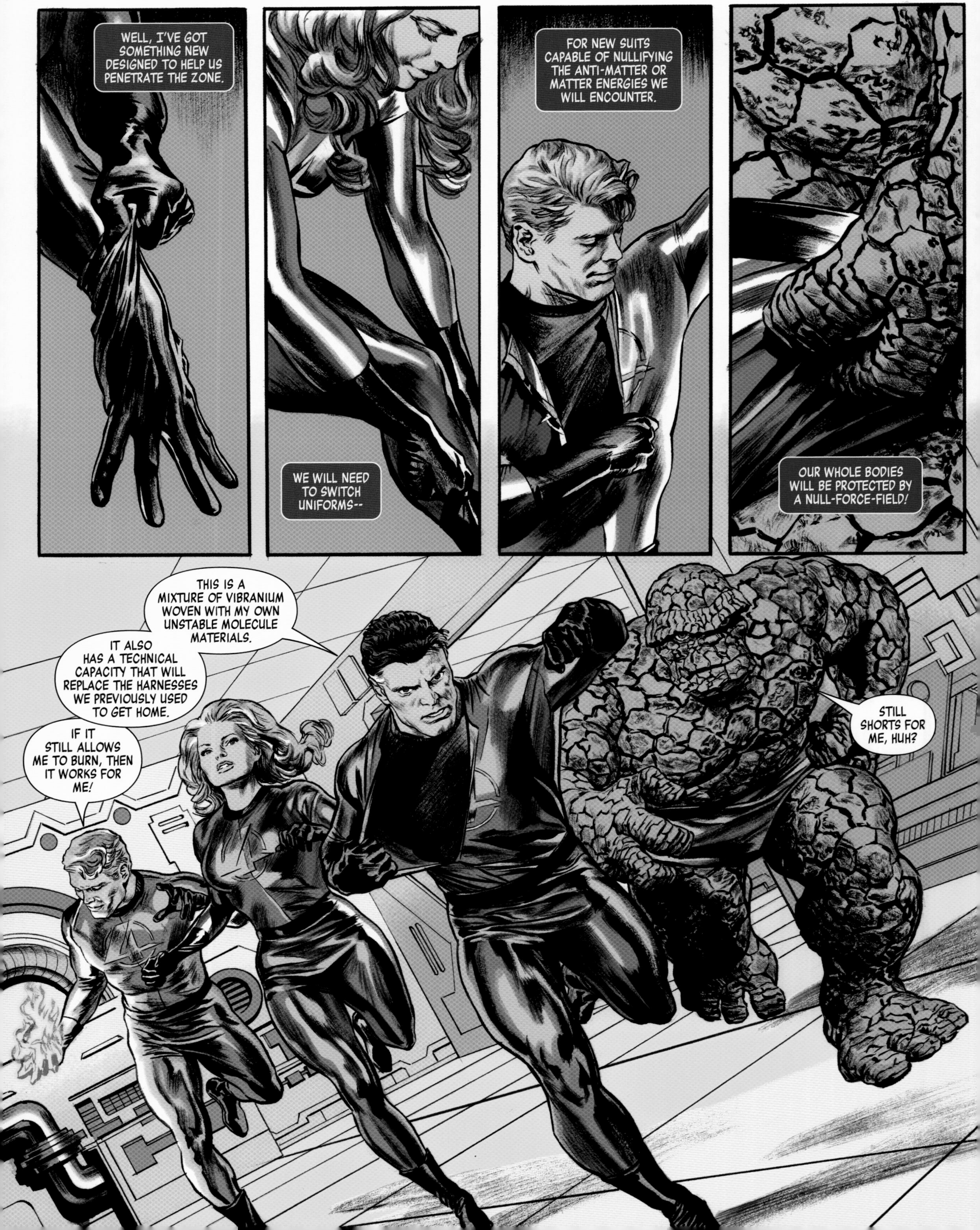
WELL, I'VE GOT SOMETHING NEW DESIGNED TO HELP US PENETRATE THE ZONE.
WE WILL NEED TO SWITCH UNIFORMS--
FOR NEW SUITS CAPABLE OF NULLIFYING THE ANTI-MATTER OR MATTER ENERGIES WE WILL ENCOUNTER.
OUR WHOLE BODIES WILL BE PROTECTED BY A NULL-FORCE-FIELD!
THIS IS A MIXTURE OF VIBRANIUM WOVEN WITH MY OWN UNSTABLE MOLECULE MATERIALS.
IT ALSO HAS A TECHNICAL CAPACITY THAT WILL REPLACE THE HARNESSES WE PREVIOUSLY USED TO GET HOME.
IF IT STILL ALLOWS ME TO BURN, THEN IT WORKS FOR ME!
STILL SHORTS FOR ME, HUH?

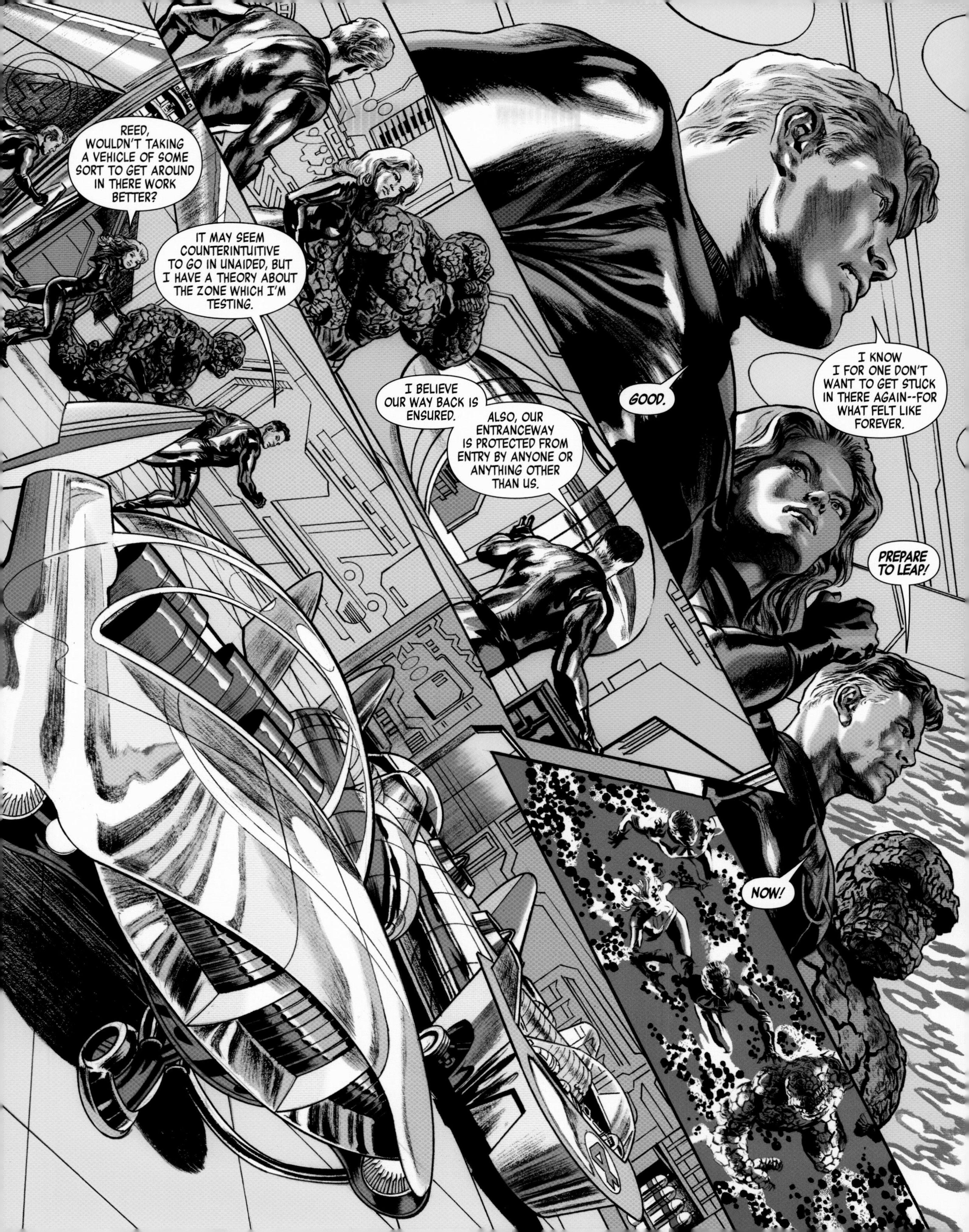
REED, WOULDN'T TAKING A VEHICLE OF SOME SORT TO GET AROUND IN THERE WORK BETTER?
IT MAY SEEM COUNTERINTUITIVE TO GO IN UNAIDED, BUT I HAVE A THEORY ABOUT THE ZONE WHICH I'M TESTING.
I BELIEVE OUR WAY BACK IS ENSURED.
ALSO, OUR ENTRANCEWAY IS PROTECTED FROM ENTRY BY ANYONE OR ANYTHING OTHER THAN US.
GOOD.
I KNOW I FOR ONE DON'T WANT TO GET STUCK IN THERE AGAIN--FOR WHAT FELT LIKE FOREVER.
PREPARE TO LEAP!
NOW!

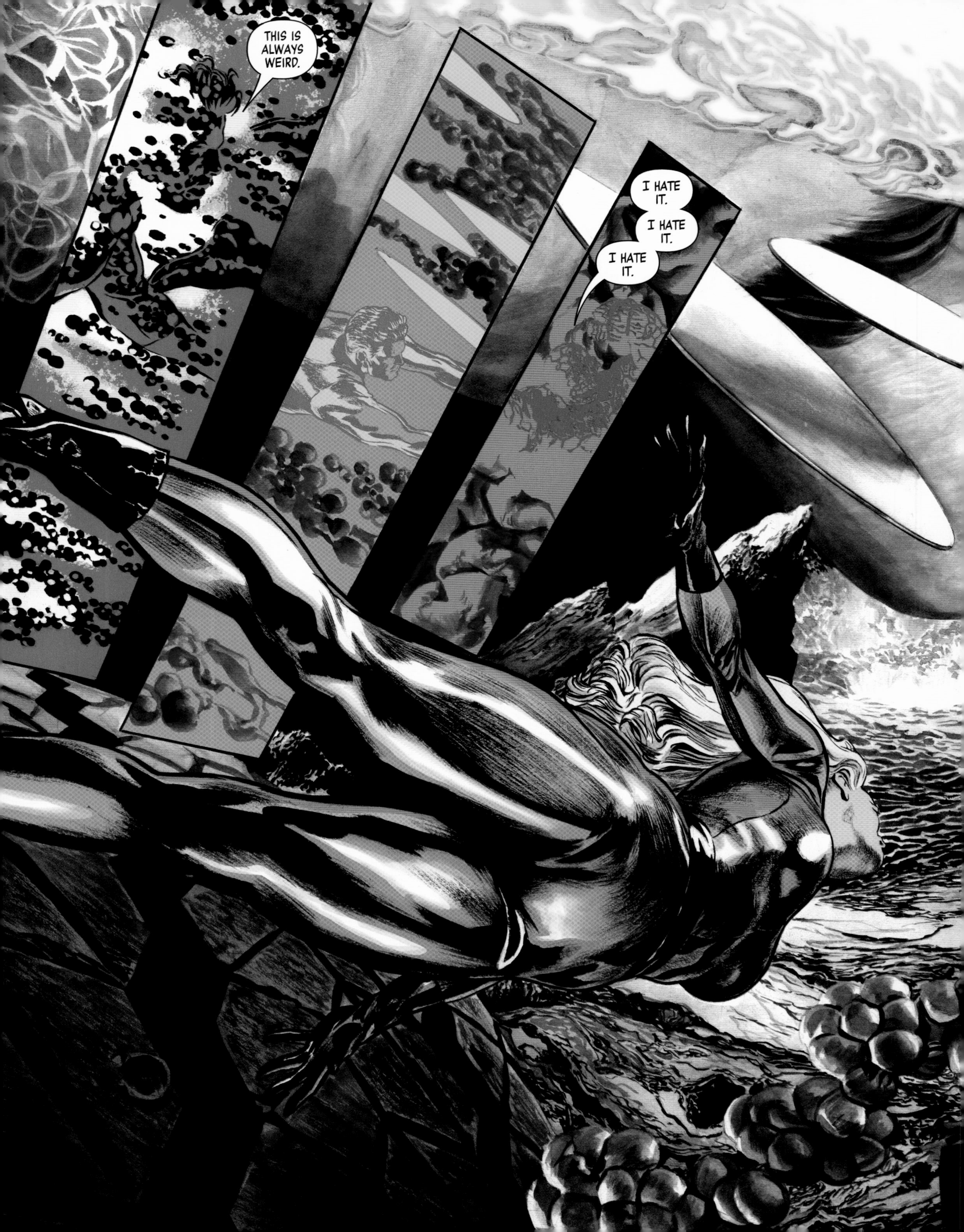
THIS IS ALWAYS WEIRD.
I HATE IT.
I HATE IT.
I HATE IT.

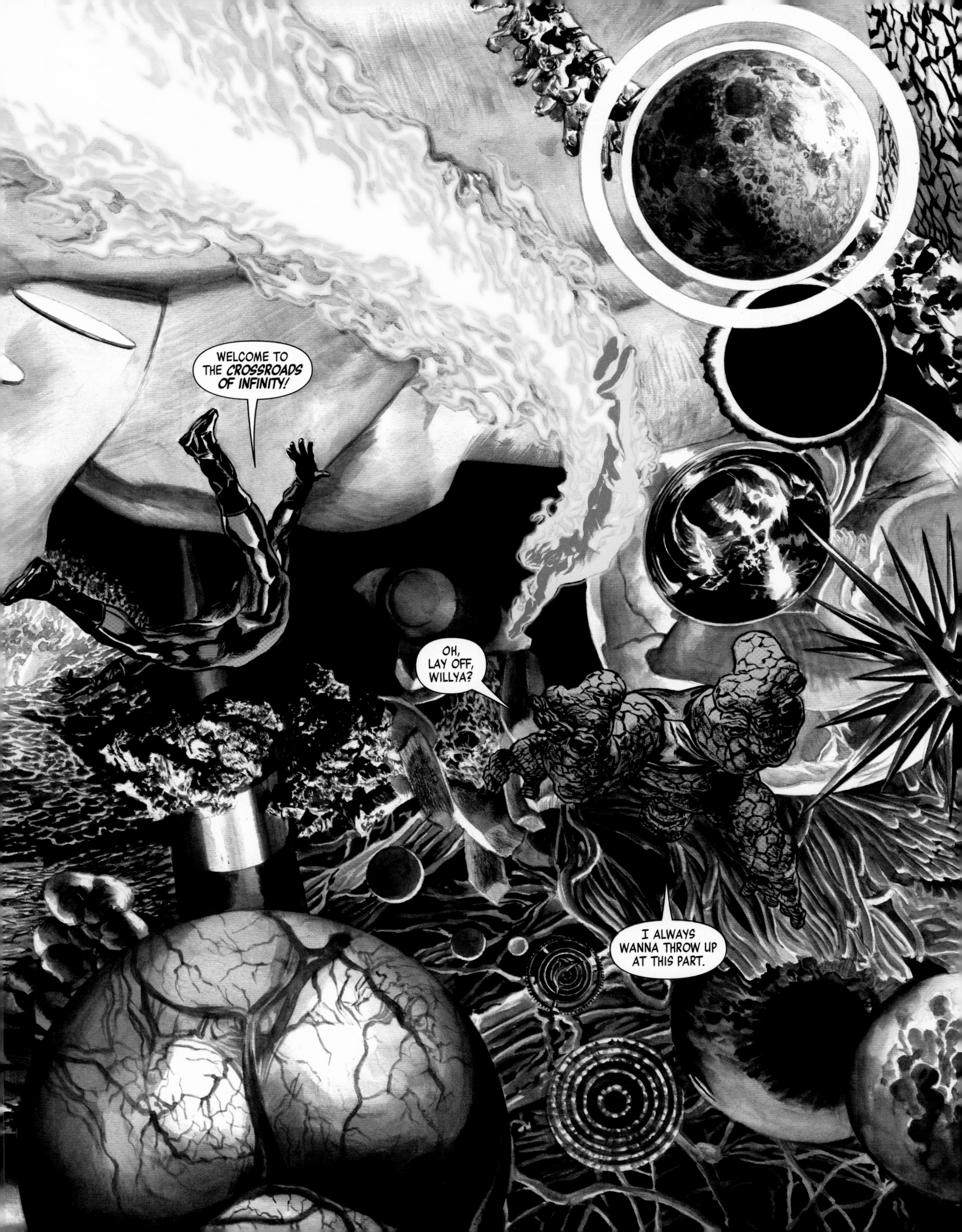
WELCOME TO THE *CROSSROADS OF INFINITY!*
OH, LAY OFF, WILLYA?
I ALWAYS WANNA THROW UP AT THIS PART.

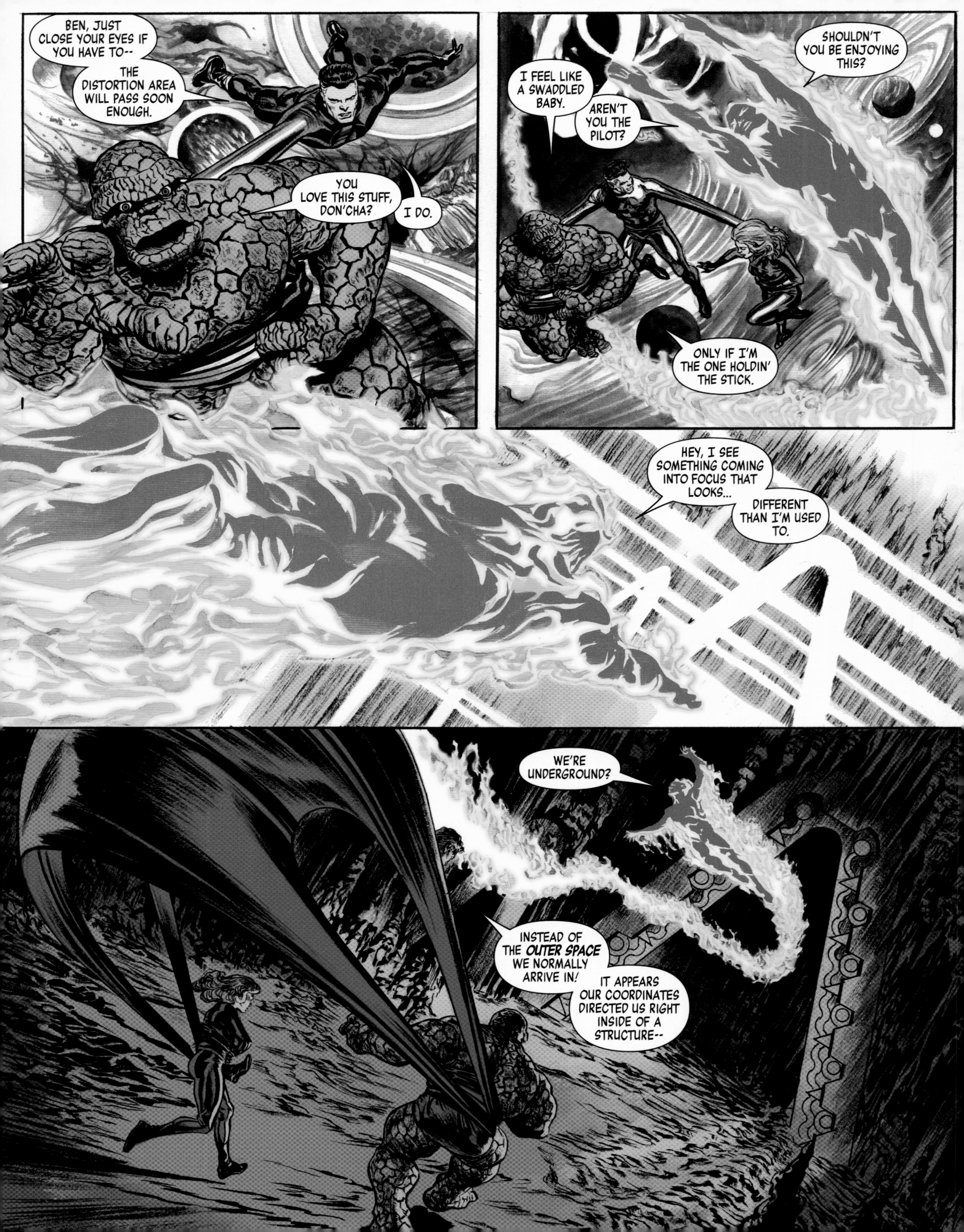
BEN, JUST CLOSE YOUR EYES IF YOU HAVE TO--
THE DISTORTION AREA WILL PASS SOON ENOUGH.
YOU LOVE THIS STUFF, DON'CHA?
I DO.
I FEEL LIKE A SWADDLED BABY.
AREN'T YOU THE PILOT?
SHOULDN'T YOU BE ENJOYING THIS?
ONLY IF I'M THE ONE HOLDIN' THE STICK.
HEY, I SEE SOMETHING COMING INTO FOCUS THAT LOOKS...
DIFFERENT THAN I'M USED TO.
WE'RE UNDERGROUND?
INSTEAD OF THE OUTER SPACE WE NORMALLY ARRIVE IN!
IT APPEARS OUR COORDINATES DIRECTED US RIGHT INSIDE OF A STRUCTURE--

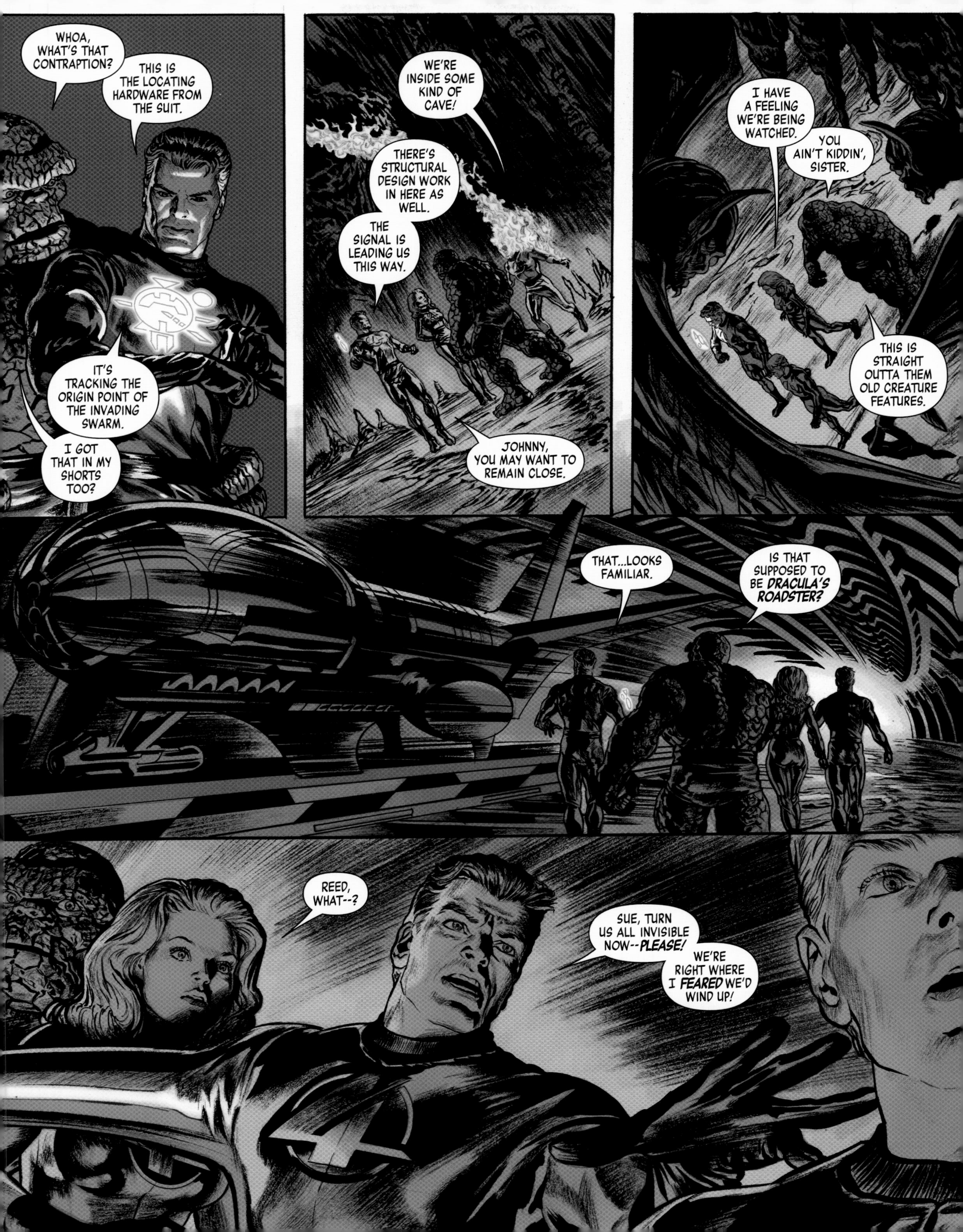
WHOA, WHAT'S THAT CONTRAPTION?
THIS IS THE LOCATING HARDWARE FROM THE SUIT.
IT'S TRACKING THE ORIGIN POINT OF THE INVADING SWARM.
I GOT THAT IN MY SHORTS TOO?
WE'RE INSIDE SOME KIND OF CAVE!
THERE'S STRUCTURAL DESIGN WORK IN HERE AS WELL.
THE SIGNAL IS LEADING US THIS WAY.
JOHNNY, YOU MAY WANT TO REMAIN CLOSE.
I HAVE A FEELING WE'RE BEING WATCHED.
YOU AIN'T KIDDIN', SISTER.
THIS IS STRAIGHT OUTTA THEM OLD CREATURE FEATURES.
THAT...LOOKS FAMILIAR.
IS THAT SUPPOSED TO BE *DRACULA'S ROADSTER?*
REED, WHAT--?
SUE, TURN US ALL INVISIBLE NOW--*PLEASE!*
WE'RE RIGHT WHERE I *FEARED* WE'D WIND UP!

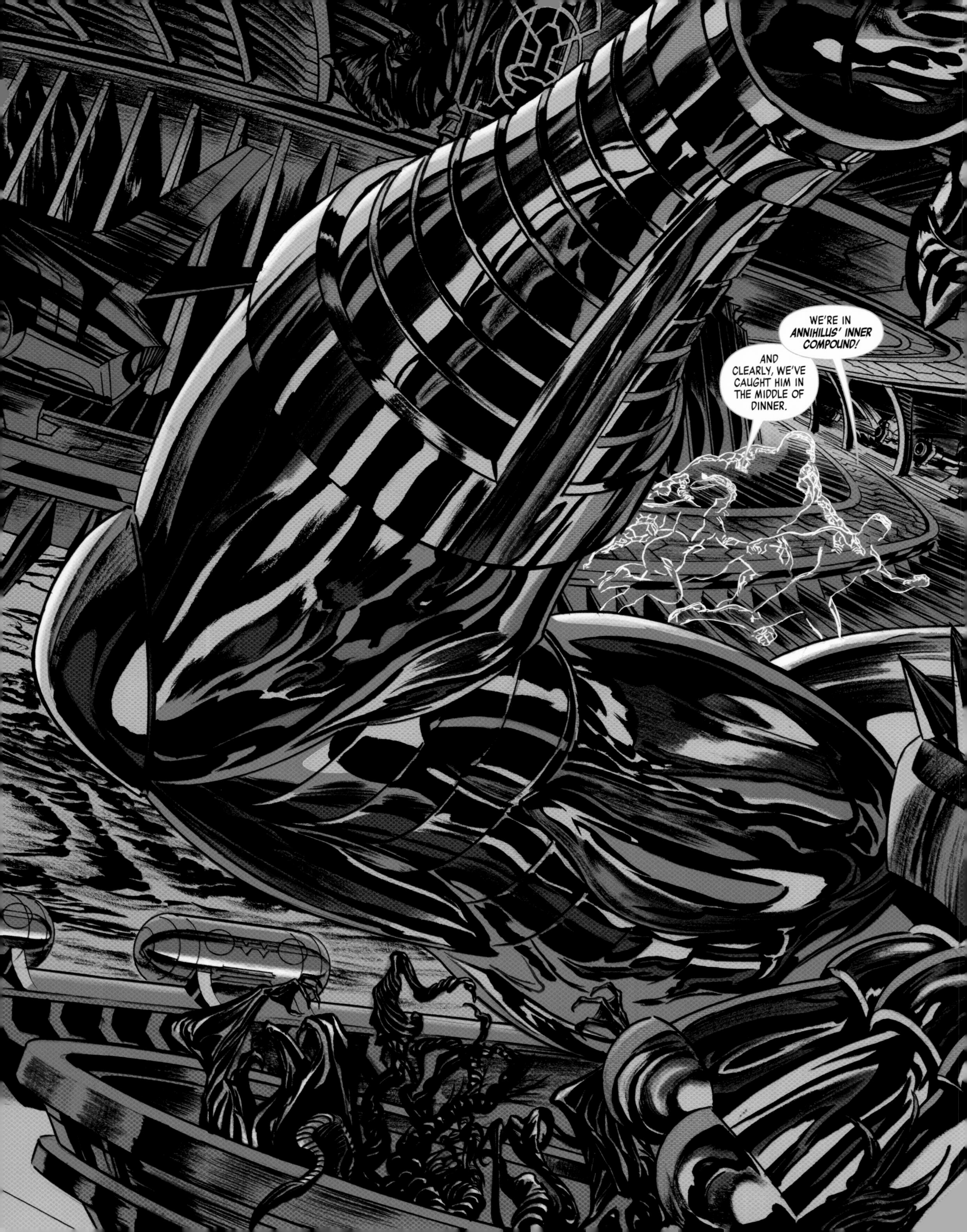
WE'RE IN ANNIHILUS' INNER COMPOUND!
AND CLEARLY, WE'VE CAUGHT HIM IN THE MIDDLE OF DINNER.

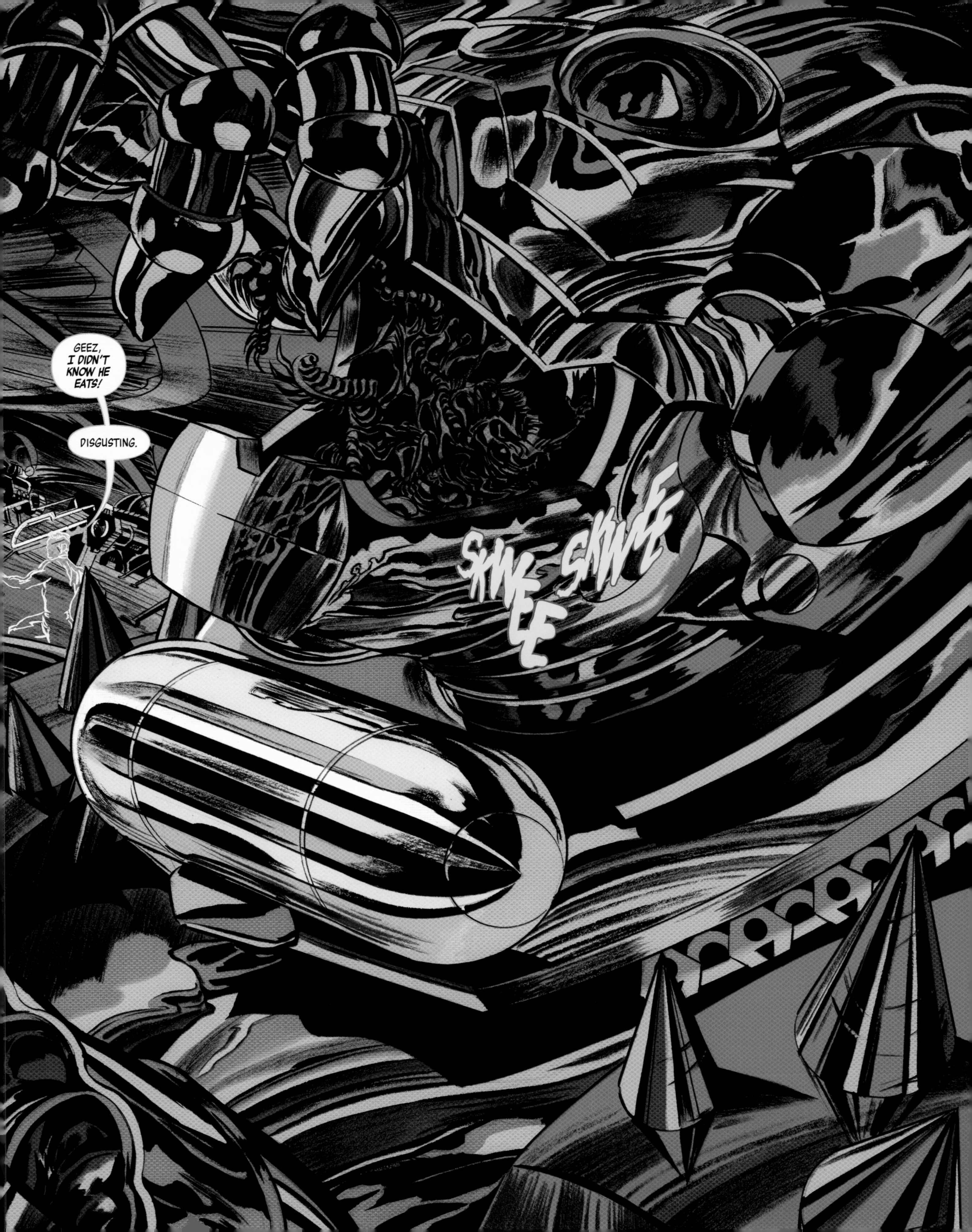
GEEZ, I DIDN'T KNOW HE EATS!
DISGUSTING.
SKWEE SKWEE

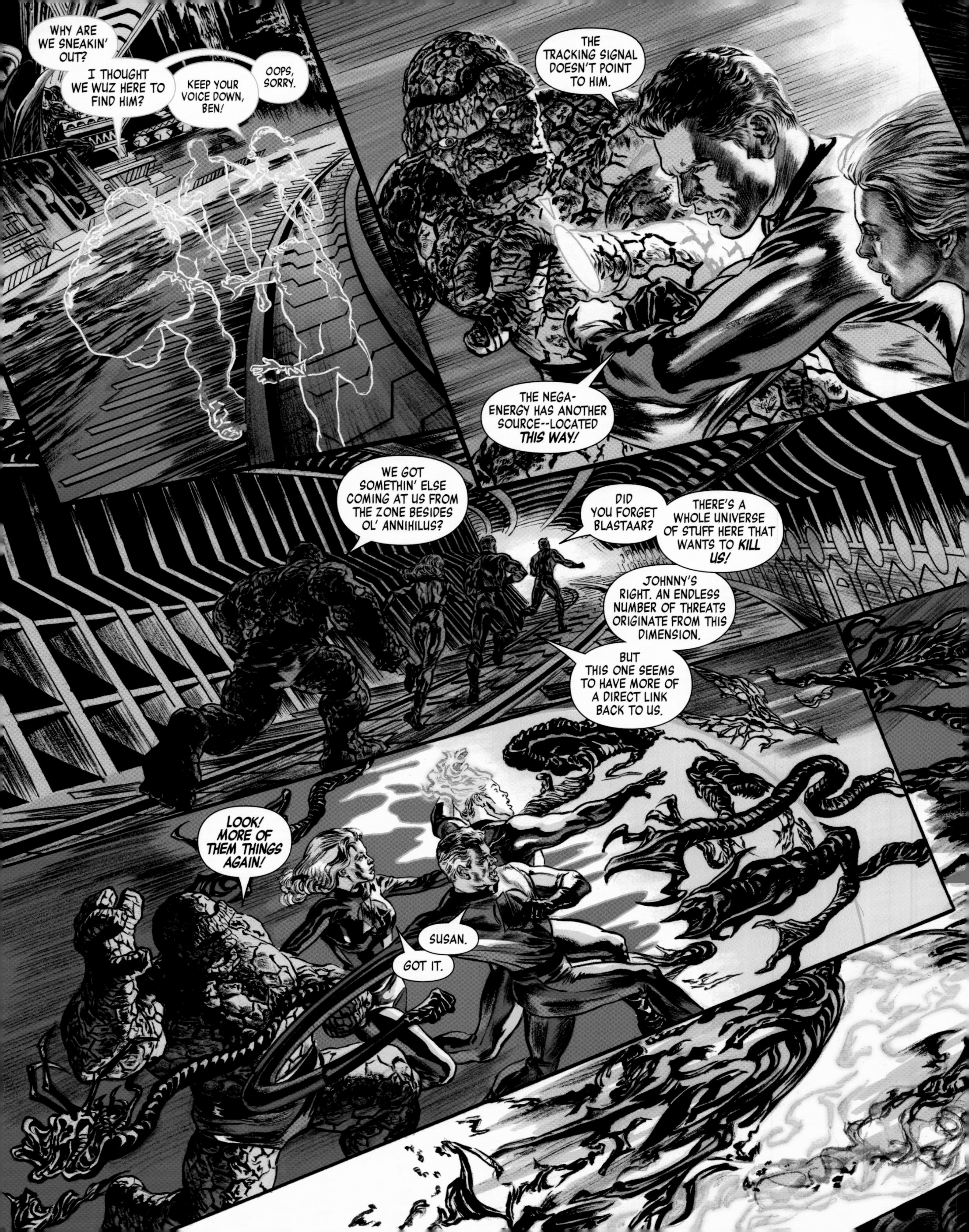

WHY ARE WE SNEAKIN' OUT?
I THOUGHT WE WUZ HERE TO FIND HIM?
KEEP YOUR VOICE DOWN, BEN!
OOPS, SORRY.
THE TRACKING SIGNAL DOESN'T POINT TO HIM.
THE NEGA-ENERGY HAS ANOTHER SOURCE--LOCATED THIS WAY!
WE GOT SOMETHIN' ELSE COMING AT US FROM THE ZONE BESIDES OL' ANNIHILUS?
DID YOU FORGET BLASTAAR?
THERE'S A WHOLE UNIVERSE OF STUFF HERE THAT WANTS TO KILL US!
JOHNNY'S RIGHT. AN ENDLESS NUMBER OF THREATS ORIGINATE FROM THIS DIMENSION.
BUT THIS ONE SEEMS TO HAVE MORE OF A DIRECT LINK BACK TO US.
LOOK! MORE OF THEM THINGS AGAIN!
SUSAN.
GOT IT.

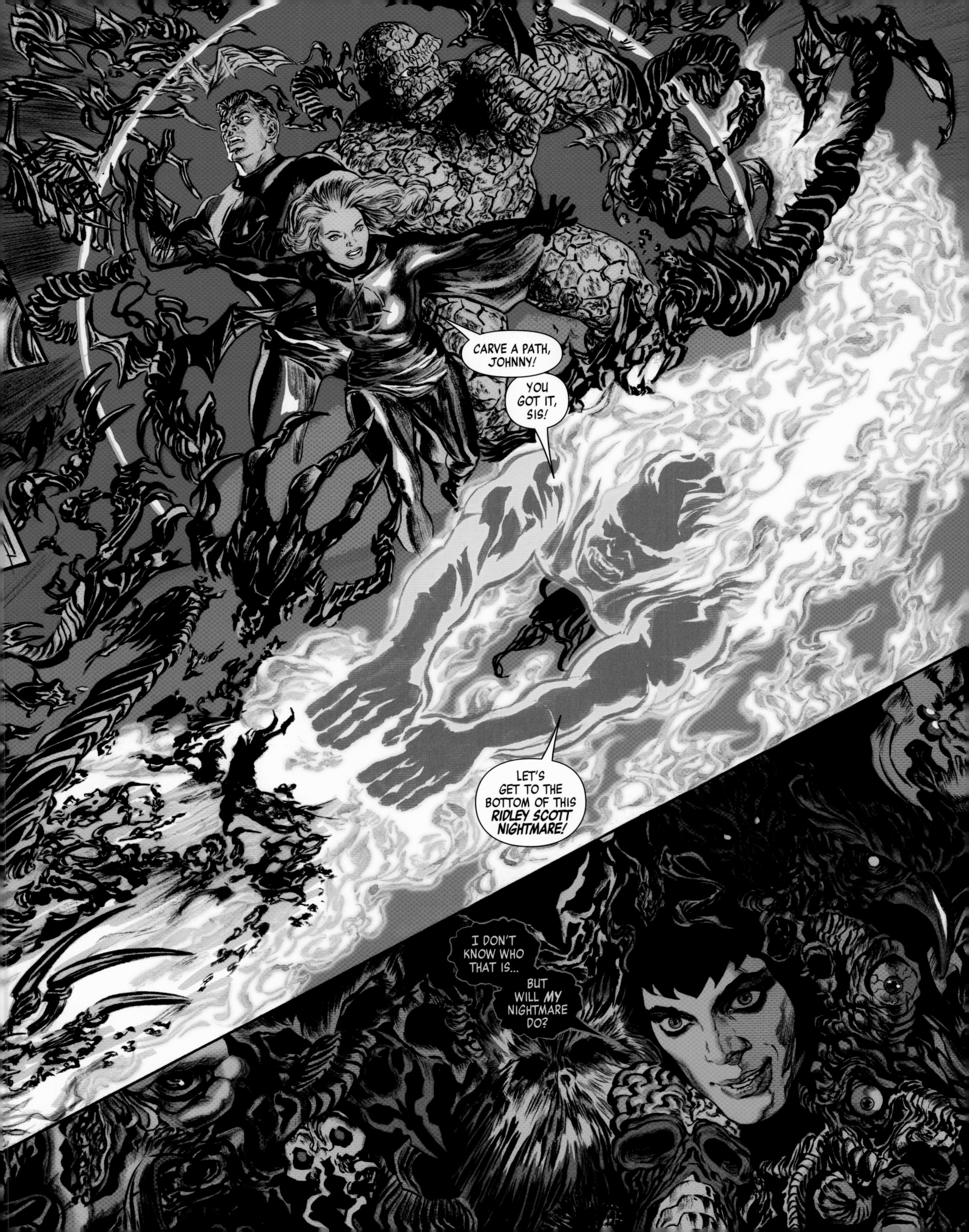
CARVE A PATH, JOHNNY!
YOU GOT IT, SIS!
LET'S GET TO THE BOTTOM OF THIS RIDLEY SCOTT NIGHTMARE!
I DON'T KNOW WHO THAT IS...
BUT WILL MY NIGHTMARE DO?

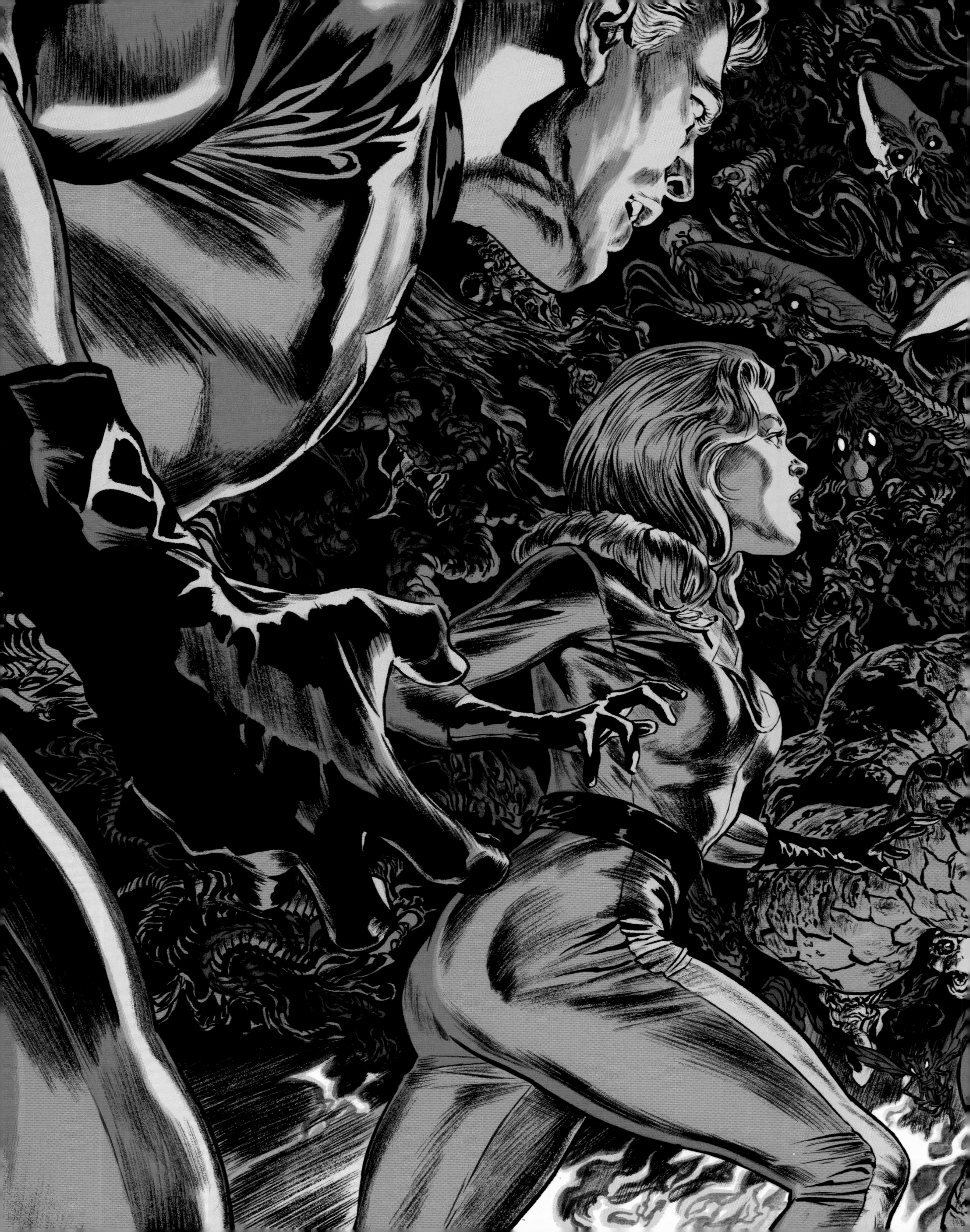

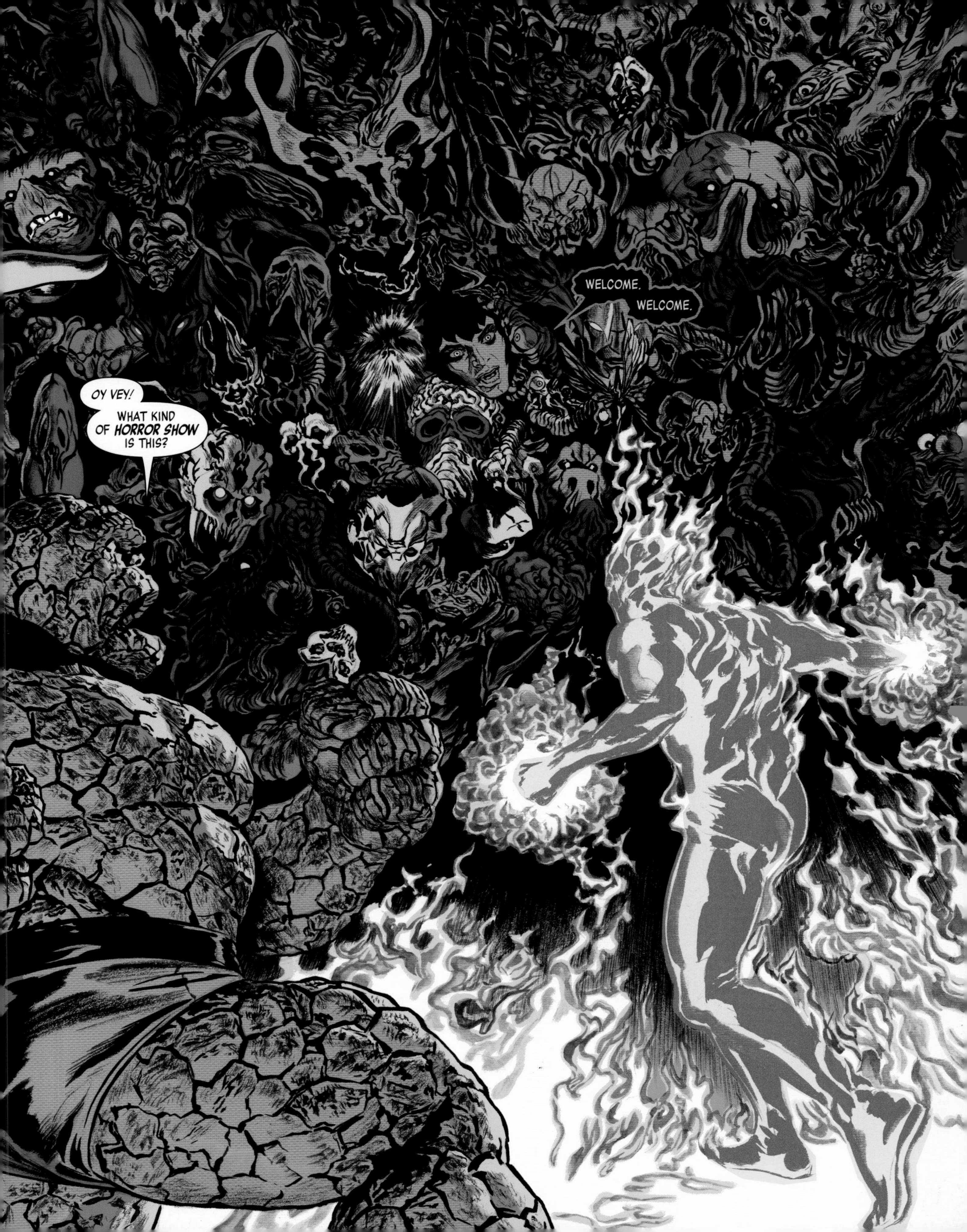
WELCOME. WELCOME.
OY VEY! WHAT KIND OF HORROR SHOW IS THIS?

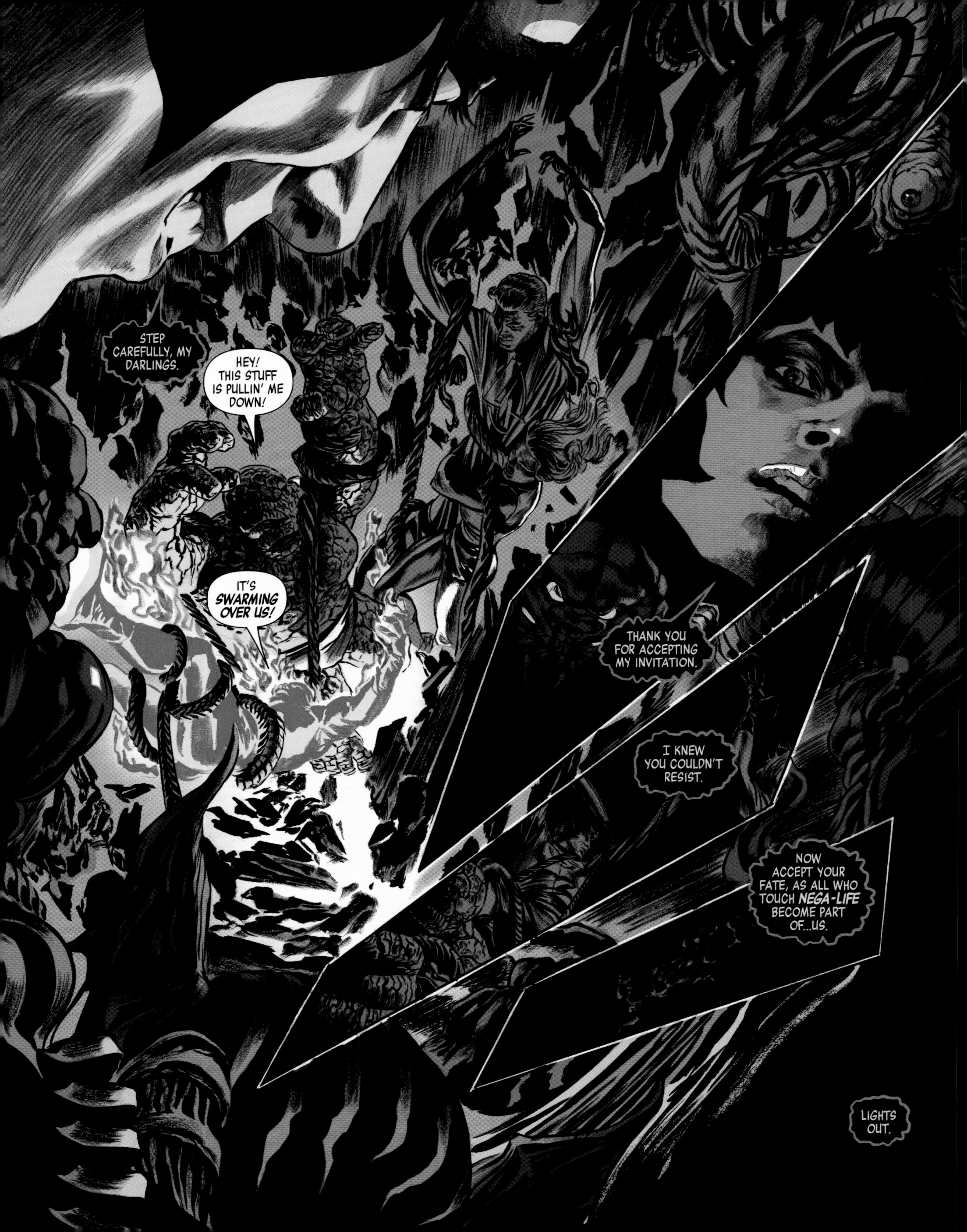
STEP CAREFULLY, MY DARLINGS.
HEY! THIS STUFF IS PULLIN' ME DOWN!
IT'S SWARMING OVER US!
THANK YOU FOR ACCEPTING MY INVITATION.
I KNEW YOU COULDN'T RESIST.
NOW ACCEPT YOUR FATE, AS ALL WHO TOUCH NEGA-LIFE BECOME PART OF...US.
LIGHTS OUT.

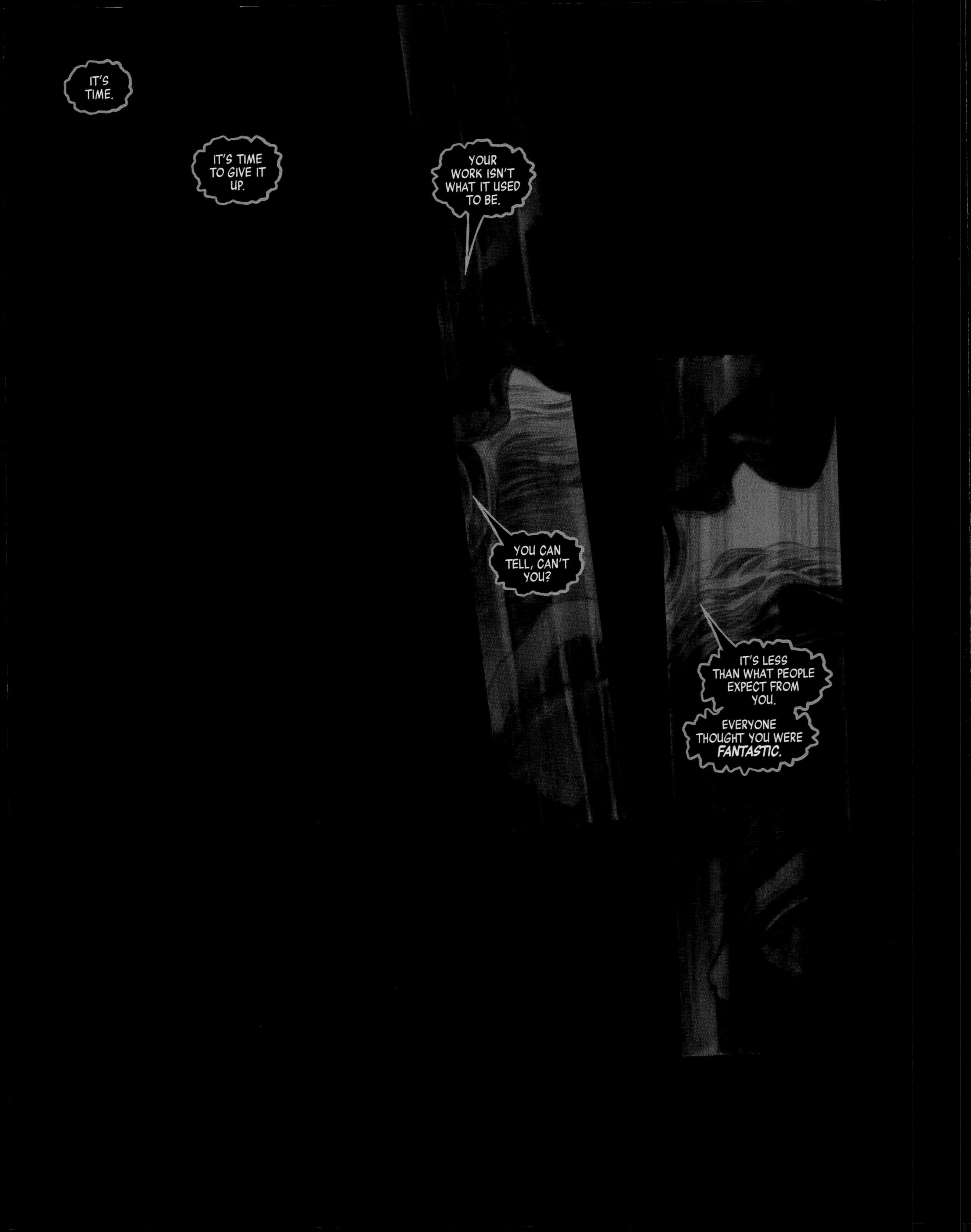

IT'S TIME.
IT'S TIME TO GIVE IT UP.
YOUR WORK ISN'T WHAT IT USED TO BE.
YOU CAN TELL, CAN'T YOU?
IT'S LESS THAN WHAT PEOPLE EXPECT FROM YOU.
EVERYONE THOUGHT YOU WERE ***FANTASTIC.***

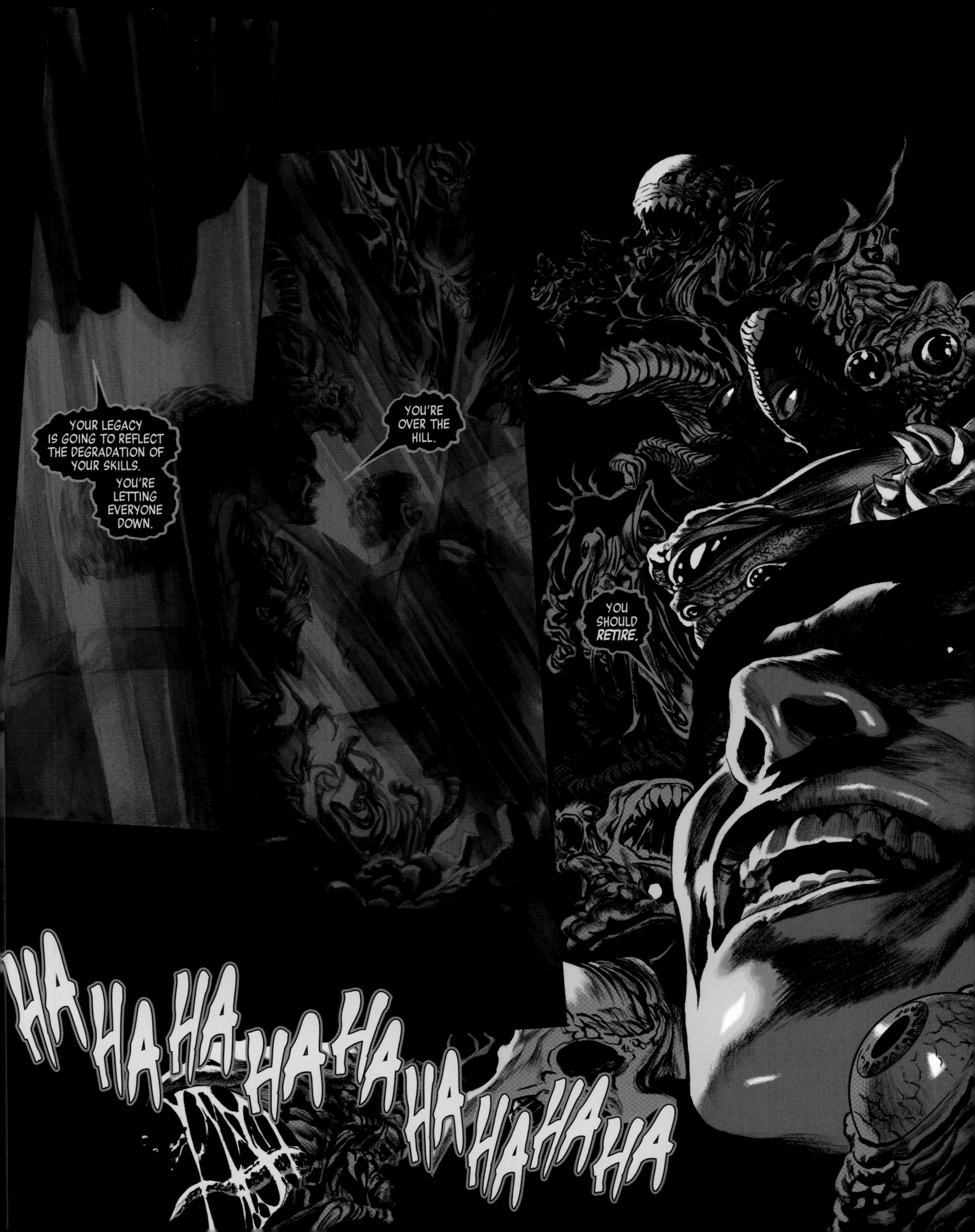
YOUR LEGACY IS GOING TO REFLECT THE DEGRADATION OF YOUR SKILLS.
YOU'RE LETTING EVERYONE DOWN.
YOU'RE OVER THE HILL.
YOU SHOULD *RETIRE*.
HA HA HA HA HA HA HA HA HA HA HA HA HA

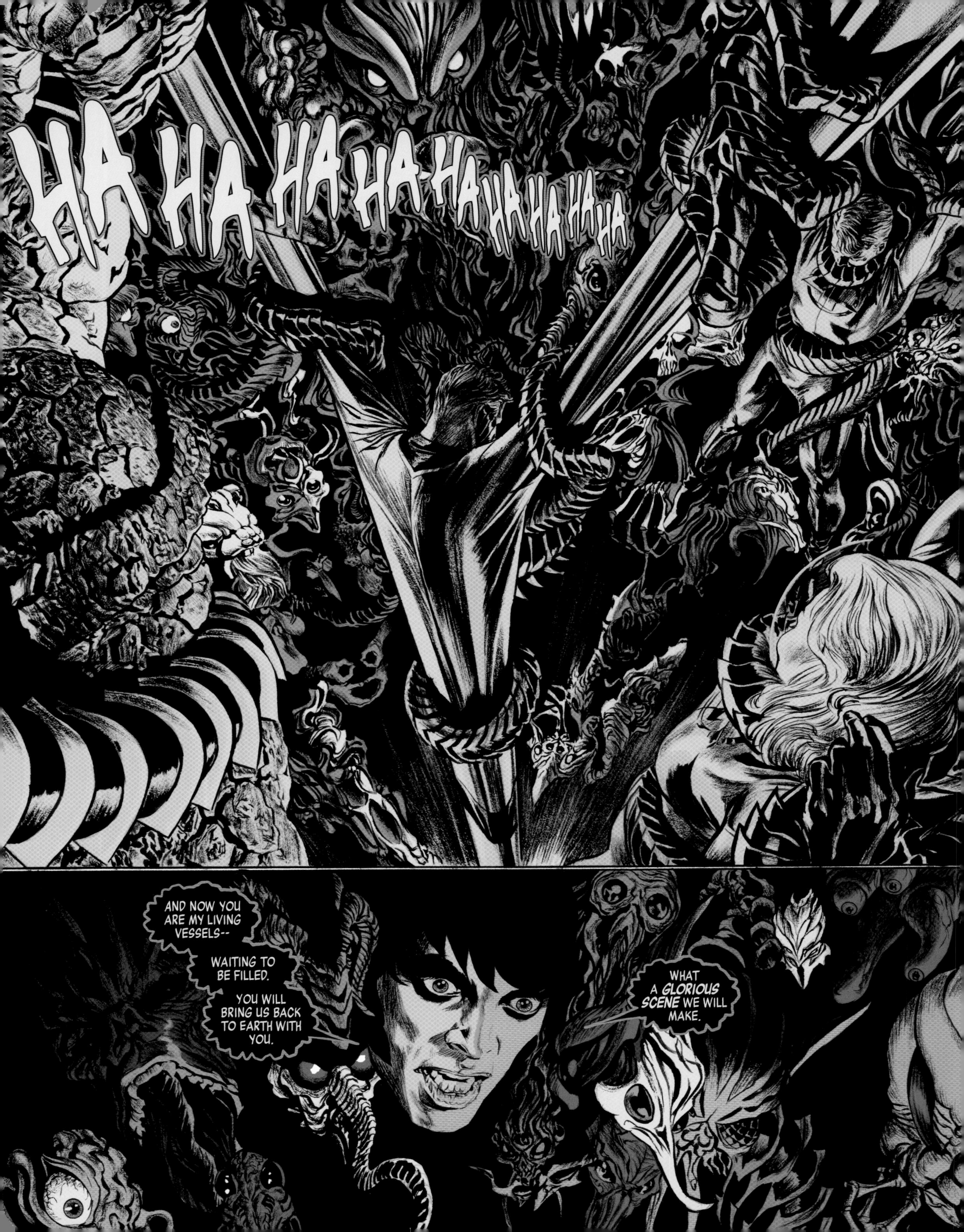
HA HA HA HA HA HA HA HA HA
AND NOW YOU ARE MY LIVING VESSELS--
WAITING TO BE FILLED.
YOU WILL BRING US BACK TO EARTH WITH YOU.
WHAT A GLORIOUS SCENE WE WILL MAKE.

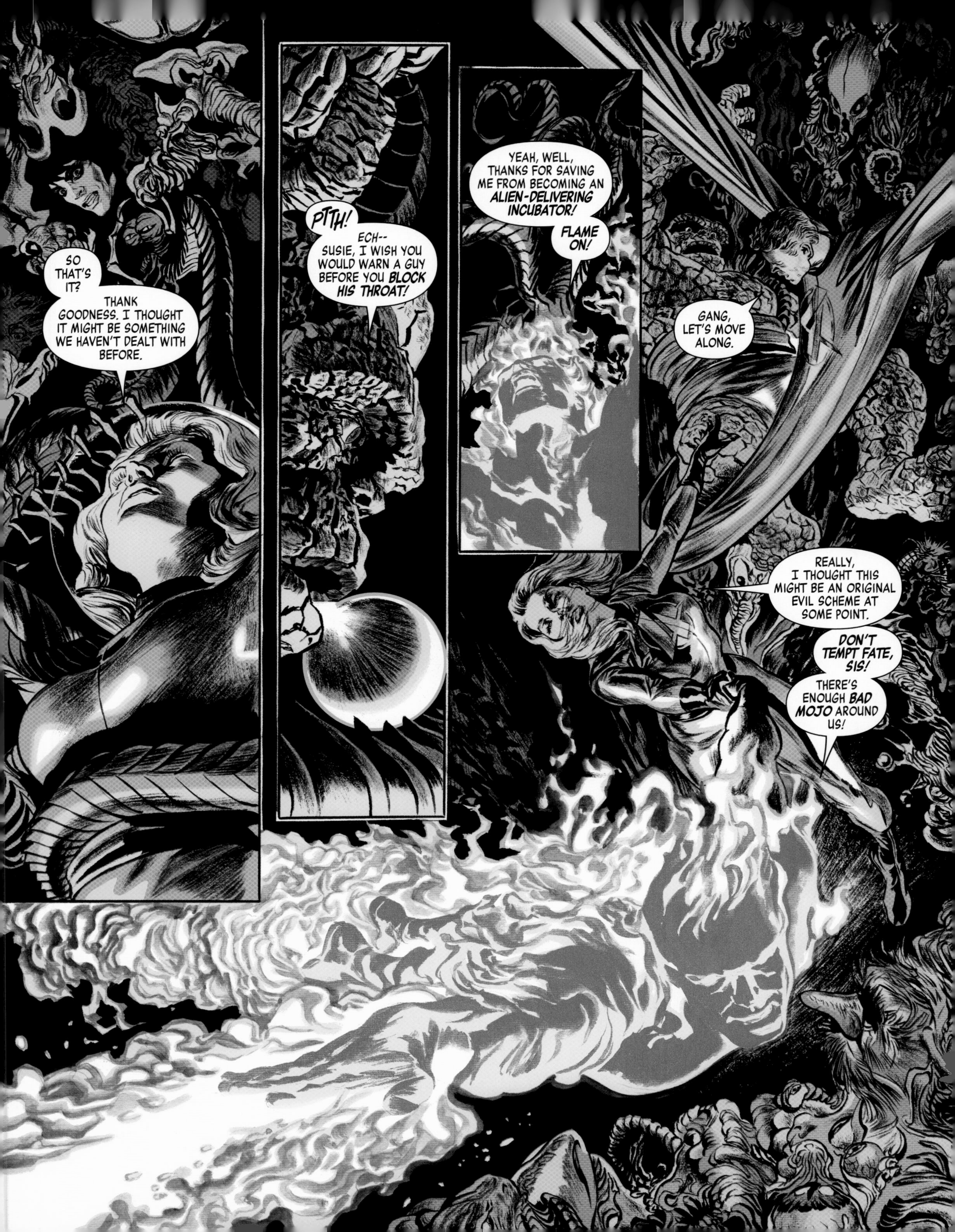
SO THAT'S IT?
THANK GOODNESS. I THOUGHT IT MIGHT BE SOMETHING WE HAVEN'T DEALT WITH BEFORE.
PTTH!
ECH-- SUSIE, I WISH YOU WOULD WARN A GUY BEFORE YOU BLOCK HIS THROAT!
YEAH, WELL, THANKS FOR SAVING ME FROM BECOMING AN ALIEN-DELIVERING INCUBATOR!
FLAME ON!
GANG, LET'S MOVE ALONG.
REALLY, I THOUGHT THIS MIGHT BE AN ORIGINAL EVIL SCHEME AT SOME POINT.
DON'T TEMPT FATE, SIS!
THERE'S ENOUGH BAD MOJO AROUND US!

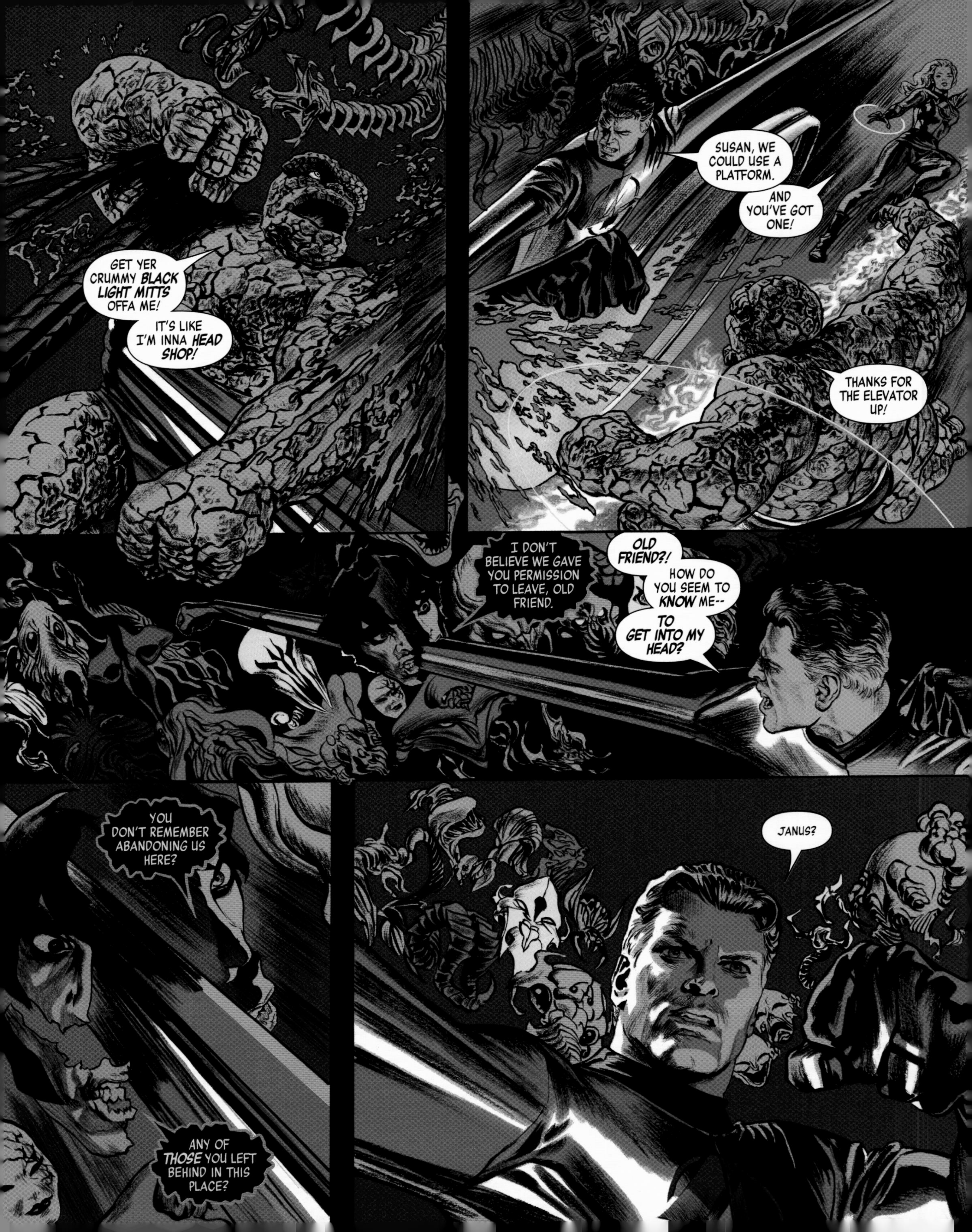
GET YER CRUMMY BLACK LIGHT MITTS OFFA ME!
IT'S LIKE I'M INNA HEAD SHOP!
SUSAN, WE COULD USE A PLATFORM.
AND YOU'VE GOT ONE!
THANKS FOR THE ELEVATOR UP!
I DON'T BELIEVE WE GAVE YOU PERMISSION TO LEAVE, OLD FRIEND.
OLD FRIEND?!
HOW DO YOU SEEM TO KNOW ME--
TO GET INTO MY HEAD?
YOU DON'T REMEMBER ABANDONING US HERE?
ANY OF THOSE YOU LEFT BEHIND IN THIS PLACE?
JANUS?

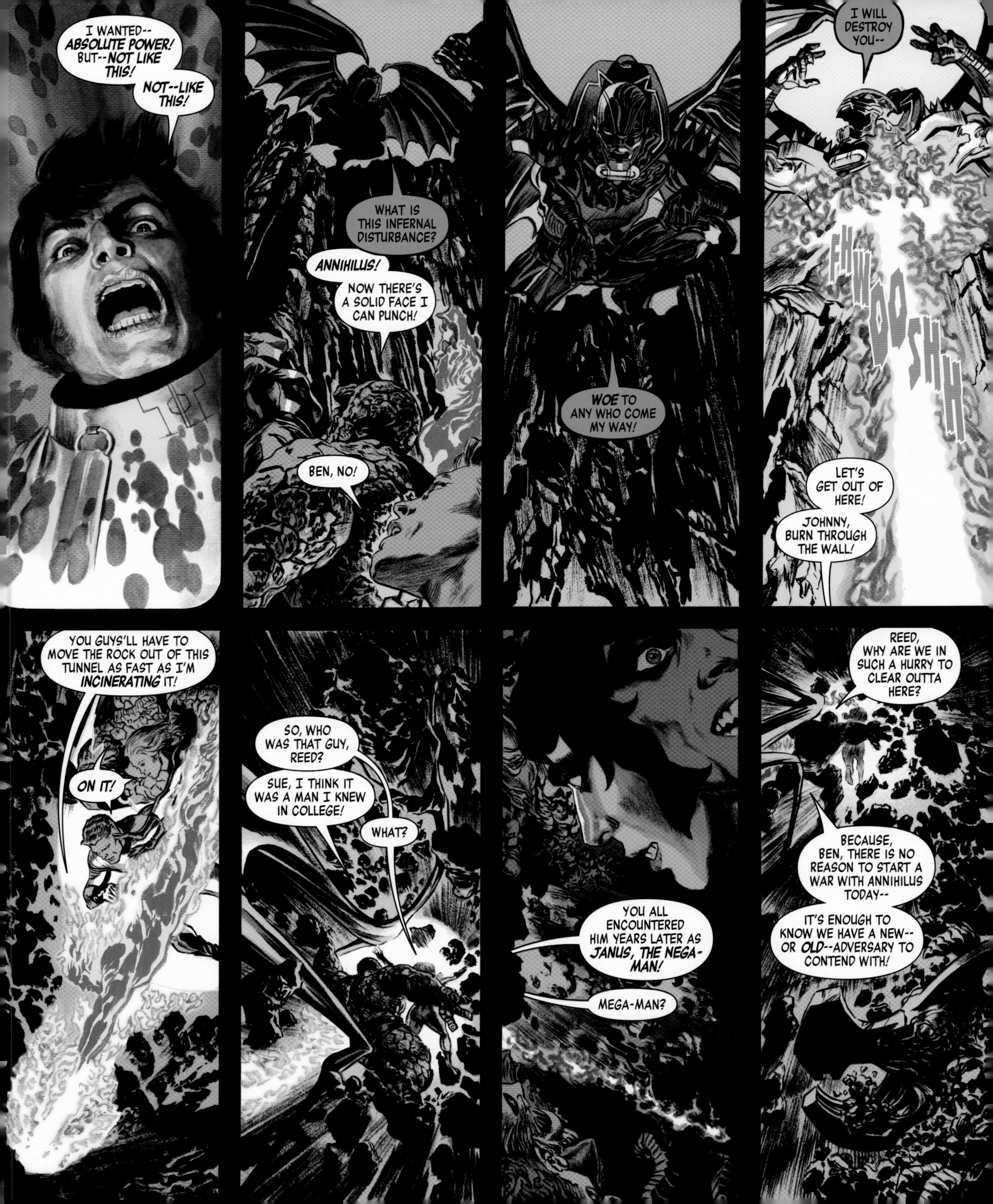
I WANTED-- ABSOLUTE POWER! BUT--NOT LIKE THIS!
NOT--LIKE THIS!
WHAT IS THIS INFERNAL DISTURBANCE?
ANNIHILUS!
NOW THERE'S A SOLID FACE I CAN PUNCH!
BEN, NO!
WOE TO ANY WHO COME MY WAY!
I WILL DESTROY YOU--
FHWOOSHH
LET'S GET OUT OF HERE!
JOHNNY, BURN THROUGH THE WALL!
YOU GUYS'LL HAVE TO MOVE THE ROCK OUT OF THIS TUNNEL AS FAST AS I'M INCINERATING IT!
ON IT!
SO, WHO WAS THAT GUY, REED?
SUE, I THINK IT WAS A MAN I KNEW IN COLLEGE!
WHAT?
YOU ALL ENCOUNTERED HIM YEARS LATER AS JANUS, THE NEGA-MAN!
MEGA-MAN?
REED, WHY ARE WE IN SUCH A HURRY TO CLEAR OUTTA HERE?
BECAUSE, BEN, THERE IS NO REASON TO START A WAR WITH ANNIHILUS TODAY--
IT'S ENOUGH TO KNOW WE HAVE A NEW-- OR OLD--ADVERSARY TO CONTEND WITH!

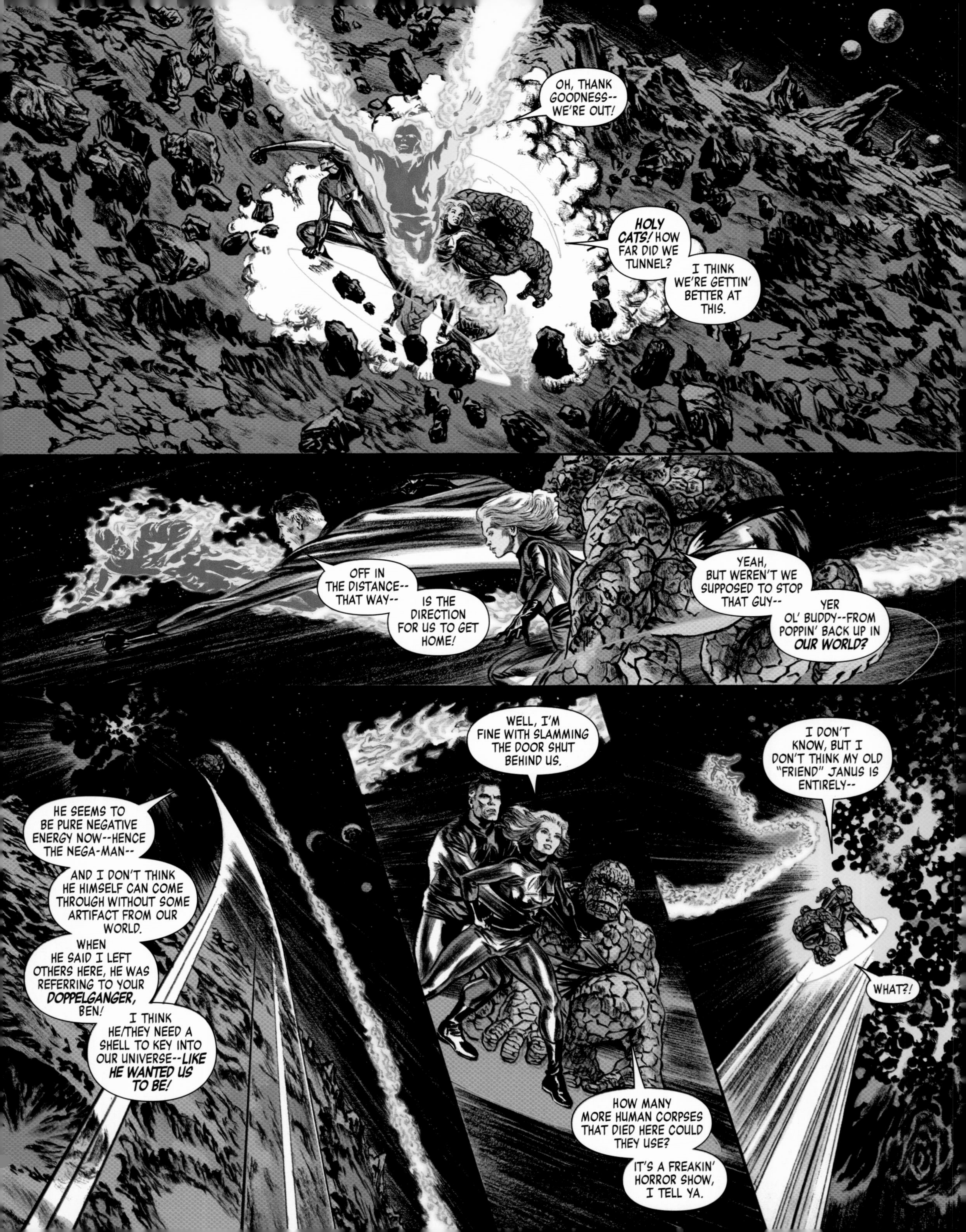
OH, THANK GOODNESS-- WE'RE OUT!
HOLY CATS! HOW FAR DID WE TUNNEL?
I THINK WE'RE GETTIN' BETTER AT THIS.
OFF IN THE DISTANCE-- THAT WAY--
IS THE DIRECTION FOR US TO GET HOME!
YEAH, BUT WEREN'T WE SUPPOSED TO STOP THAT GUY--
YER OL' BUDDY--FROM POPPIN' BACK UP IN OUR WORLD?
HE SEEMS TO BE PURE NEGATIVE ENERGY NOW--HENCE THE NEGA-MAN--
AND I DON'T THINK HE HIMSELF CAN COME THROUGH WITHOUT SOME ARTIFACT FROM OUR WORLD.
WHEN HE SAID I LEFT OTHERS HERE, HE WAS REFERRING TO YOUR DOPPELGANGER, BEN!
I THINK HE/THEY NEED A SHELL TO KEY INTO OUR UNIVERSE--LIKE HE WANTED US TO BE!
WELL, I'M FINE WITH SLAMMING THE DOOR SHUT BEHIND US.
HOW MANY MORE HUMAN CORPSES THAT DIED HERE COULD THEY USE?
IT'S A FREAKIN' HORROR SHOW, I TELL YA.
I DON'T KNOW, BUT I DON'T THINK MY OLD "FRIEND" JANUS IS ENTIRELY--
WHAT?!

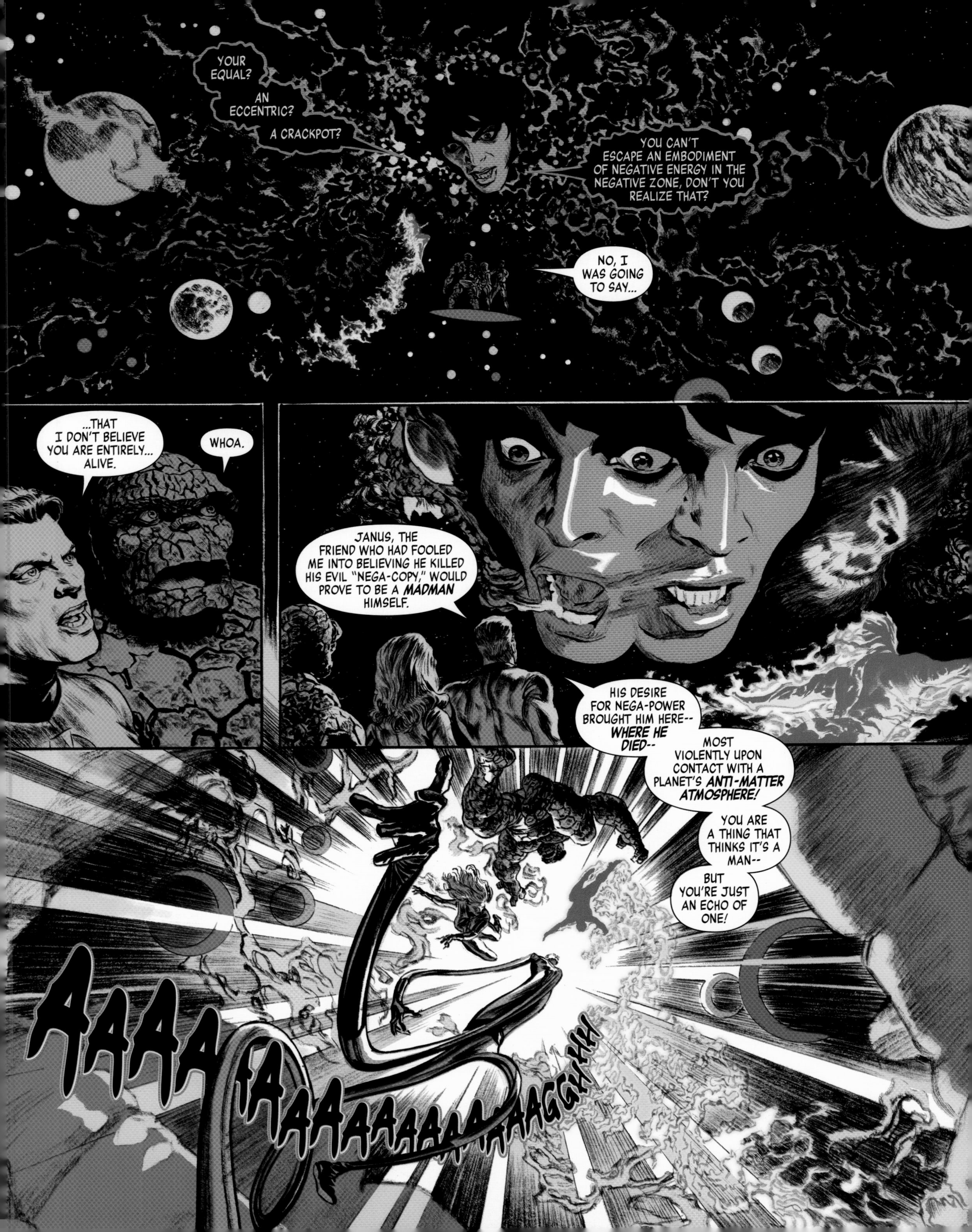
YOUR EQUAL?
AN ECCENTRIC?
A CRACKPOT?
YOU CAN'T ESCAPE AN EMBODIMENT OF NEGATIVE ENERGY IN THE NEGATIVE ZONE, DON'T YOU REALIZE THAT?
NO, I WAS GOING TO SAY...
...THAT I DON'T BELIEVE YOU ARE ENTIRELY... ALIVE.
WHOA.
JANUS, THE FRIEND WHO HAD FOOLED ME INTO BELIEVING HE KILLED HIS EVIL "NEGA-COPY," WOULD PROVE TO BE A ***MADMAN*** HIMSELF.
HIS DESIRE FOR NEGA-POWER BROUGHT HIM HERE-- ***WHERE HE DIED***--
MOST VIOLENTLY UPON CONTACT WITH A PLANET'S ***ANTI-MATTER ATMOSPHERE!***
YOU ARE A THING THAT THINKS IT'S A MAN--
BUT YOU'RE JUST AN ECHO OF ONE!
AAAAAAAAAAAAAAAAAAGGHHH

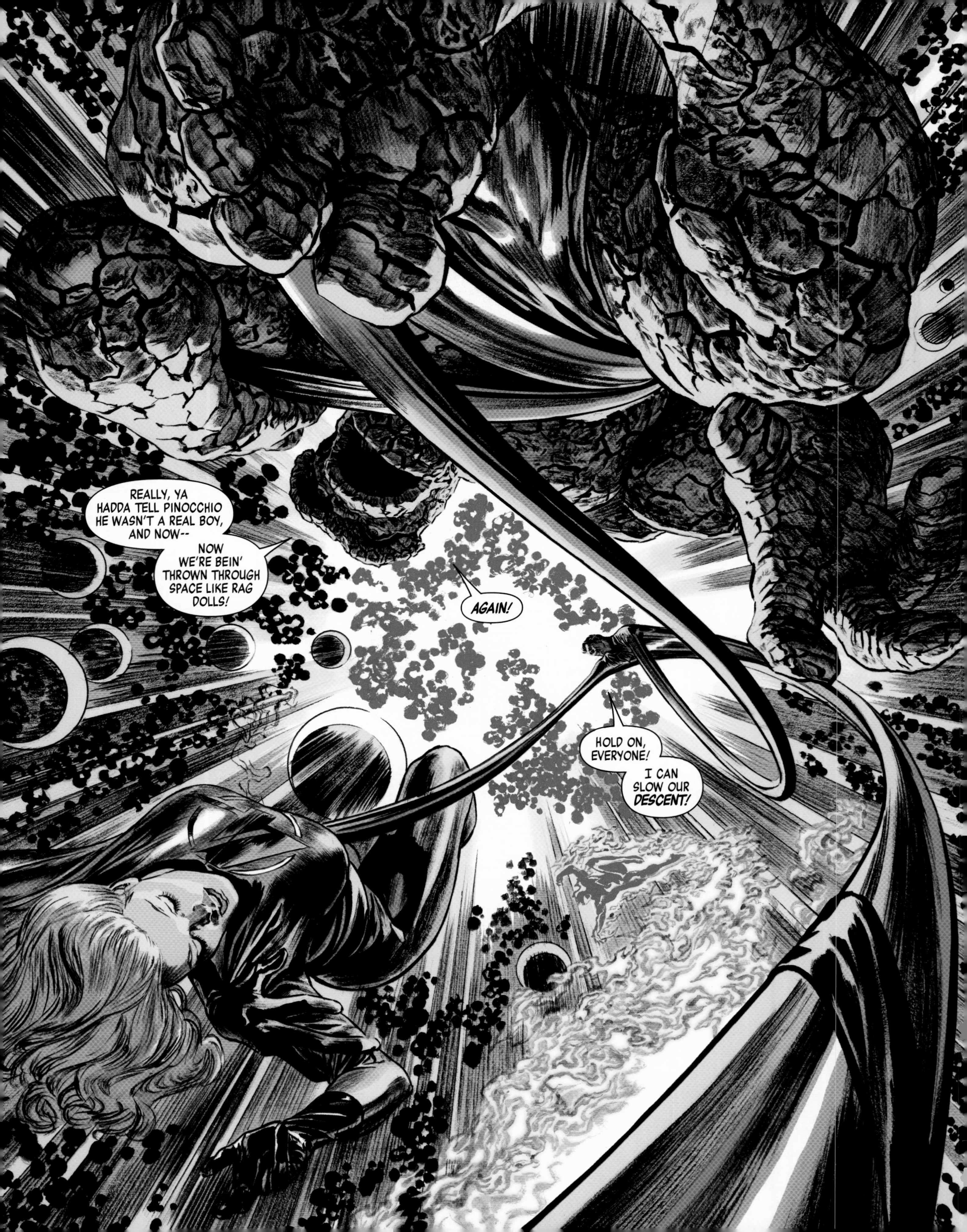
REALLY, YA HADDA TELL PINOCCHIO HE WASN'T A REAL BOY, AND NOW--
NOW WE'RE BEIN' THROWN THROUGH SPACE LIKE RAG DOLLS!
AGAIN!
HOLD ON, EVERYONE!
I CAN SLOW OUR DESCENT!

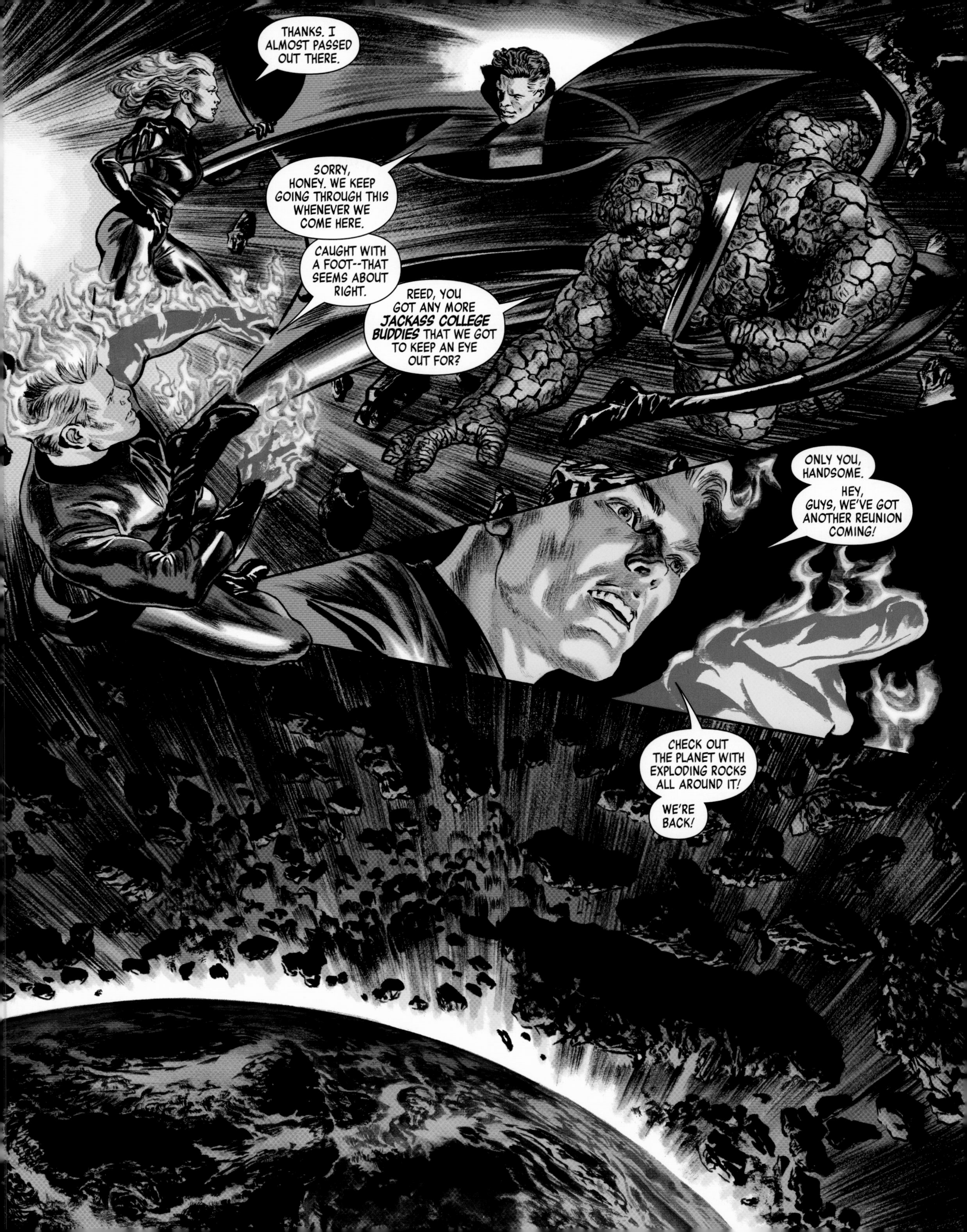
THANKS. I ALMOST PASSED OUT THERE.
SORRY, HONEY. WE KEEP GOING THROUGH THIS WHENEVER WE COME HERE.
CAUGHT WITH A FOOT--THAT SEEMS ABOUT RIGHT.
REED, YOU GOT ANY MORE JACKASS COLLEGE BUDDIES THAT WE GOT TO KEEP AN EYE OUT FOR?
ONLY YOU, HANDSOME.
HEY, GUYS, WE'VE GOT ANOTHER REUNION COMING!
CHECK OUT THE PLANET WITH EXPLODING ROCKS ALL AROUND IT!
WE'RE BACK!

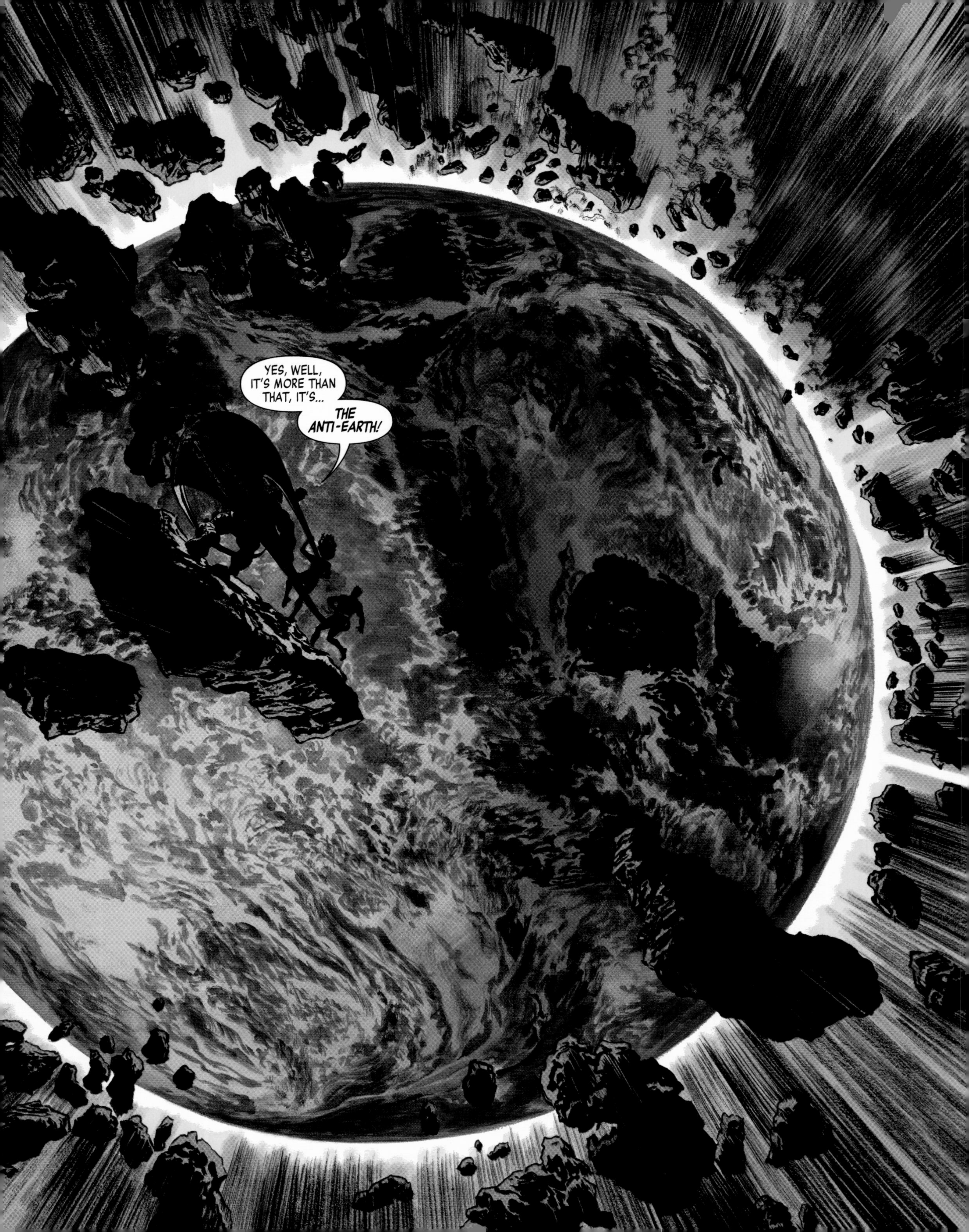
YES, WELL, IT'S MORE THAN THAT, IT'S... THE ANTI-EARTH!

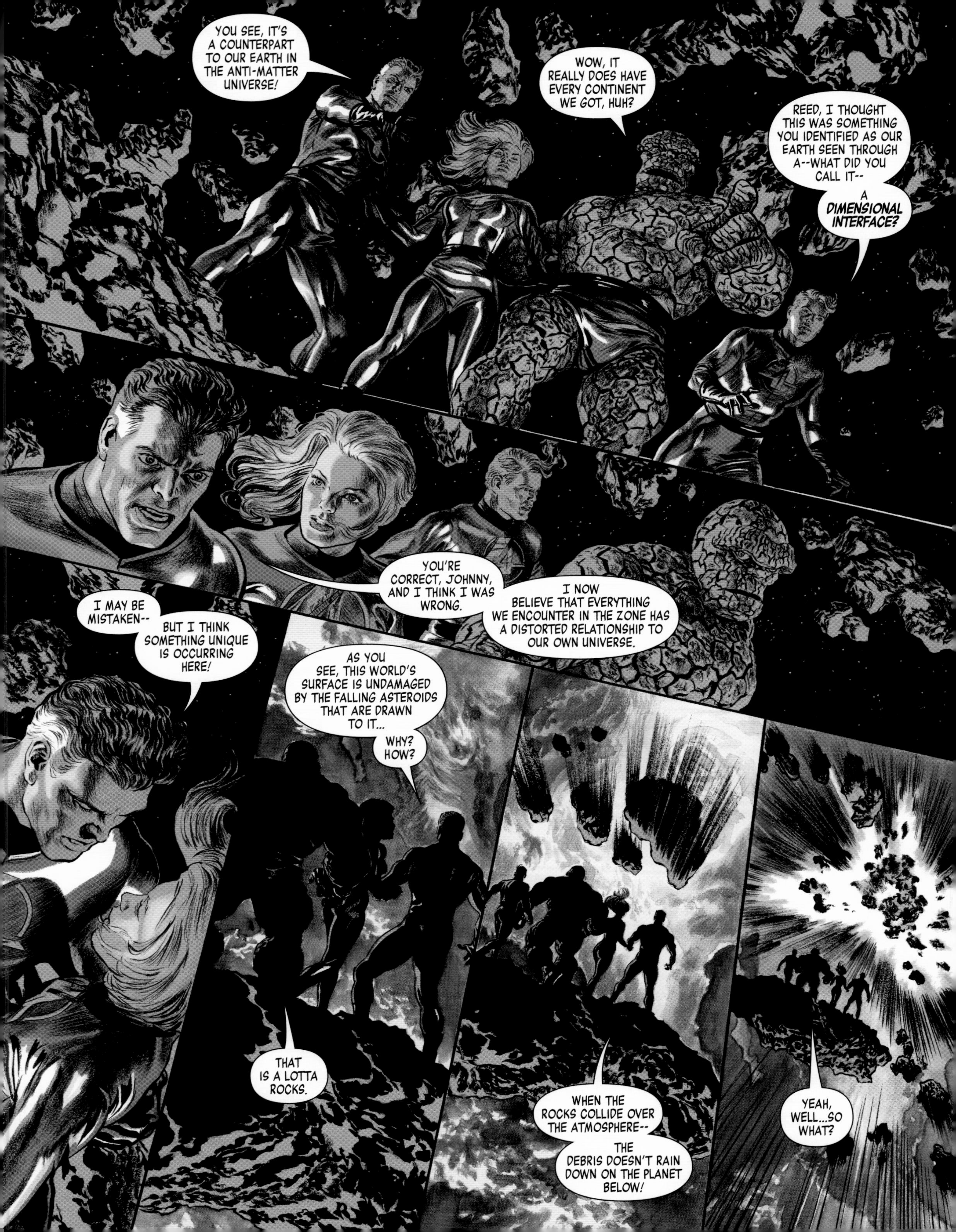
YOU SEE, IT'S A COUNTERPART TO OUR EARTH IN THE ANTI-MATTER UNIVERSE!
WOW, IT REALLY DOES HAVE EVERY CONTINENT WE GOT, HUH?
REED, I THOUGHT THIS WAS SOMETHING YOU IDENTIFIED AS OUR EARTH SEEN THROUGH A--WHAT DID YOU CALL IT--
A *DIMENSIONAL INTERFACE?*
YOU'RE CORRECT, JOHNNY, AND I THINK I WAS WRONG.
I NOW BELIEVE THAT EVERYTHING WE ENCOUNTER IN THE ZONE HAS A DISTORTED RELATIONSHIP TO OUR OWN UNIVERSE.
I MAY BE MISTAKEN--
BUT I THINK SOMETHING UNIQUE IS OCCURRING HERE!
AS YOU SEE, THIS WORLD'S SURFACE IS UNDAMAGED BY THE FALLING ASTEROIDS THAT ARE DRAWN TO IT...
WHY? HOW?
THAT IS A LOTTA ROCKS.
WHEN THE ROCKS COLLIDE OVER THE ATMOSPHERE--
THE DEBRIS DOESN'T RAIN DOWN ON THE PLANET BELOW!
YEAH, WELL...SO WHAT?

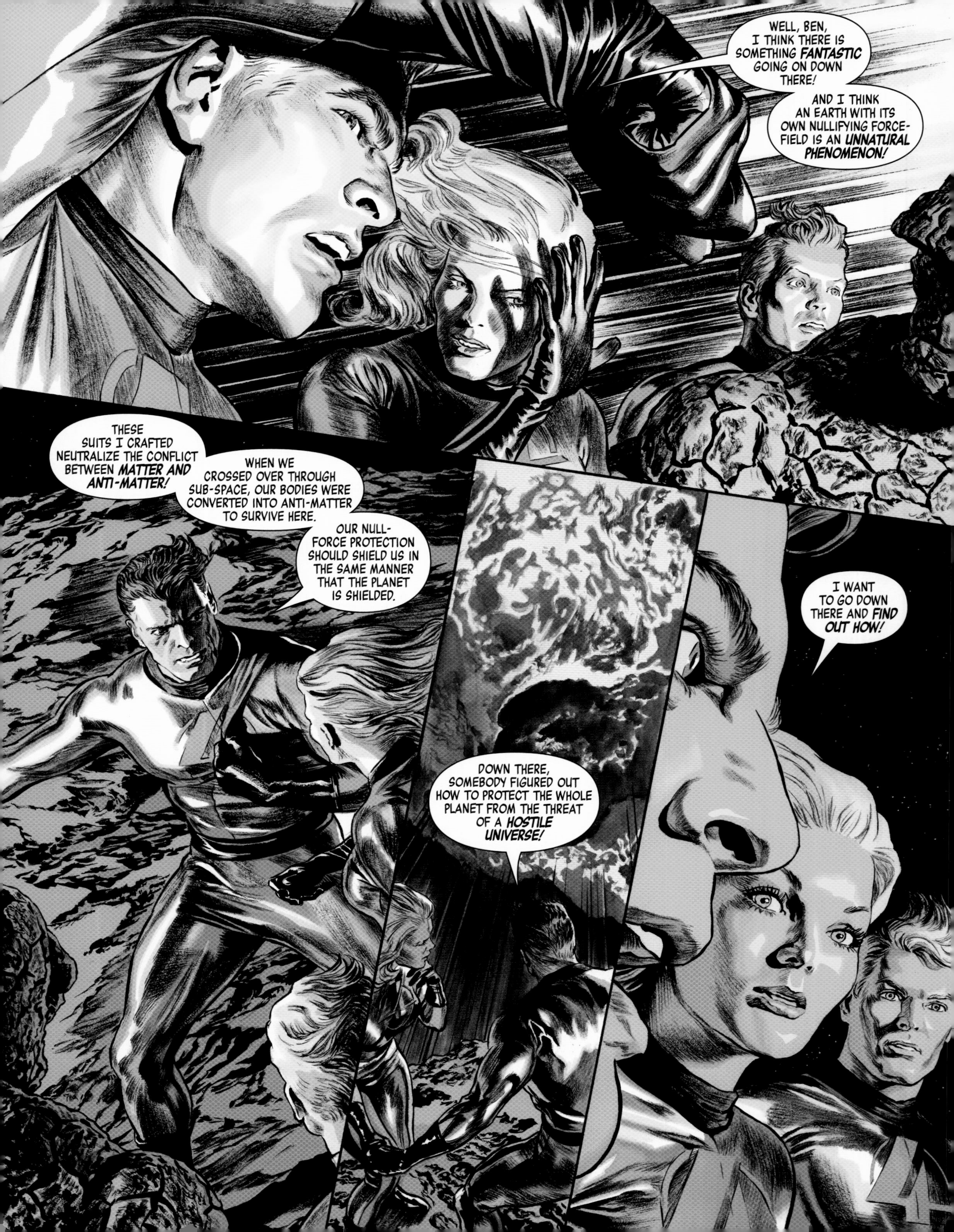
WELL, BEN, I THINK THERE IS SOMETHING FANTASTIC GOING ON DOWN THERE!
AND I THINK AN EARTH WITH ITS OWN NULLIFYING FORCE-FIELD IS AN UNNATURAL PHENOMENON!
THESE SUITS I CRAFTED NEUTRALIZE THE CONFLICT BETWEEN MATTER AND ANTI-MATTER!
WHEN WE CROSSED OVER THROUGH SUB-SPACE, OUR BODIES WERE CONVERTED INTO ANTI-MATTER TO SURVIVE HERE.
OUR NULL-FORCE PROTECTION SHOULD SHIELD US IN THE SAME MANNER THAT THE PLANET IS SHIELDED.
DOWN THERE, SOMEBODY FIGURED OUT HOW TO PROTECT THE WHOLE PLANET FROM THE THREAT OF A HOSTILE UNIVERSE!
I WANT TO GO DOWN THERE AND FIND OUT HOW!

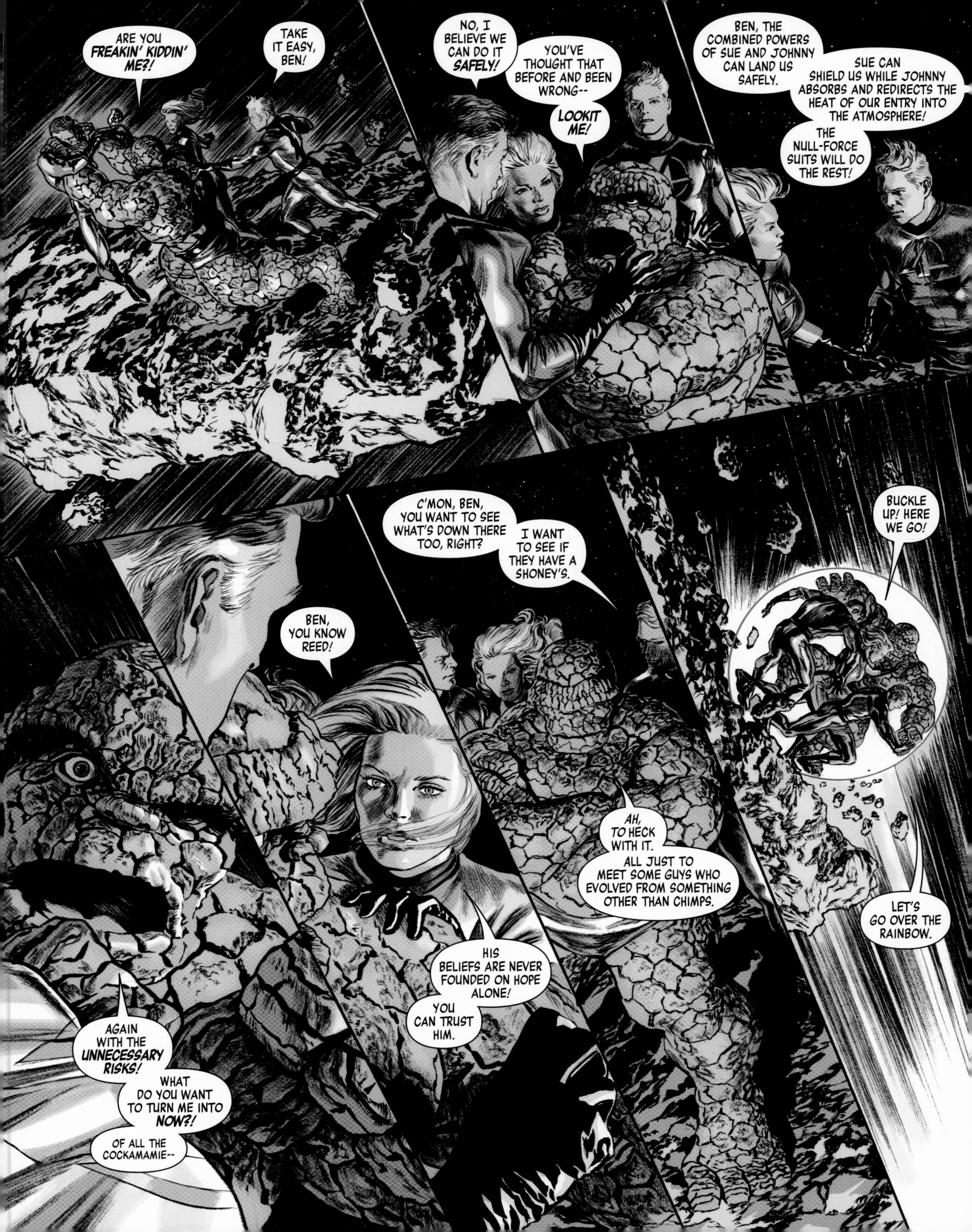
ARE YOU FREAKIN' KIDDIN' ME?!
TAKE IT EASY, BEN!
NO, I BELIEVE WE CAN DO IT SAFELY!
YOU'VE THOUGHT THAT BEFORE AND BEEN WRONG--
LOOKIT ME!
BEN, THE COMBINED POWERS OF SUE AND JOHNNY CAN LAND US SAFELY.
SUE CAN SHIELD US WHILE JOHNNY ABSORBS AND REDIRECTS THE HEAT OF OUR ENTRY INTO THE ATMOSPHERE!
THE NULL-FORCE SUITS WILL DO THE REST!
AGAIN WITH THE UNNECESSARY RISKS!
WHAT DO YOU WANT TO TURN ME INTO NOW?!
OF ALL THE COCKAMAMIE--
BEN, YOU KNOW REED!
HIS BELIEFS ARE NEVER FOUNDED ON HOPE ALONE!
YOU CAN TRUST HIM.
C'MON, BEN, YOU WANT TO SEE WHAT'S DOWN THERE TOO, RIGHT?
I WANT TO SEE IF THEY HAVE A SHONEY'S.
AH, TO HECK WITH IT.
ALL JUST TO MEET SOME GUYS WHO EVOLVED FROM SOMETHING OTHER THAN CHIMPS.
BUCKLE UP! HERE WE GO!
LET'S GO OVER THE RAINBOW.

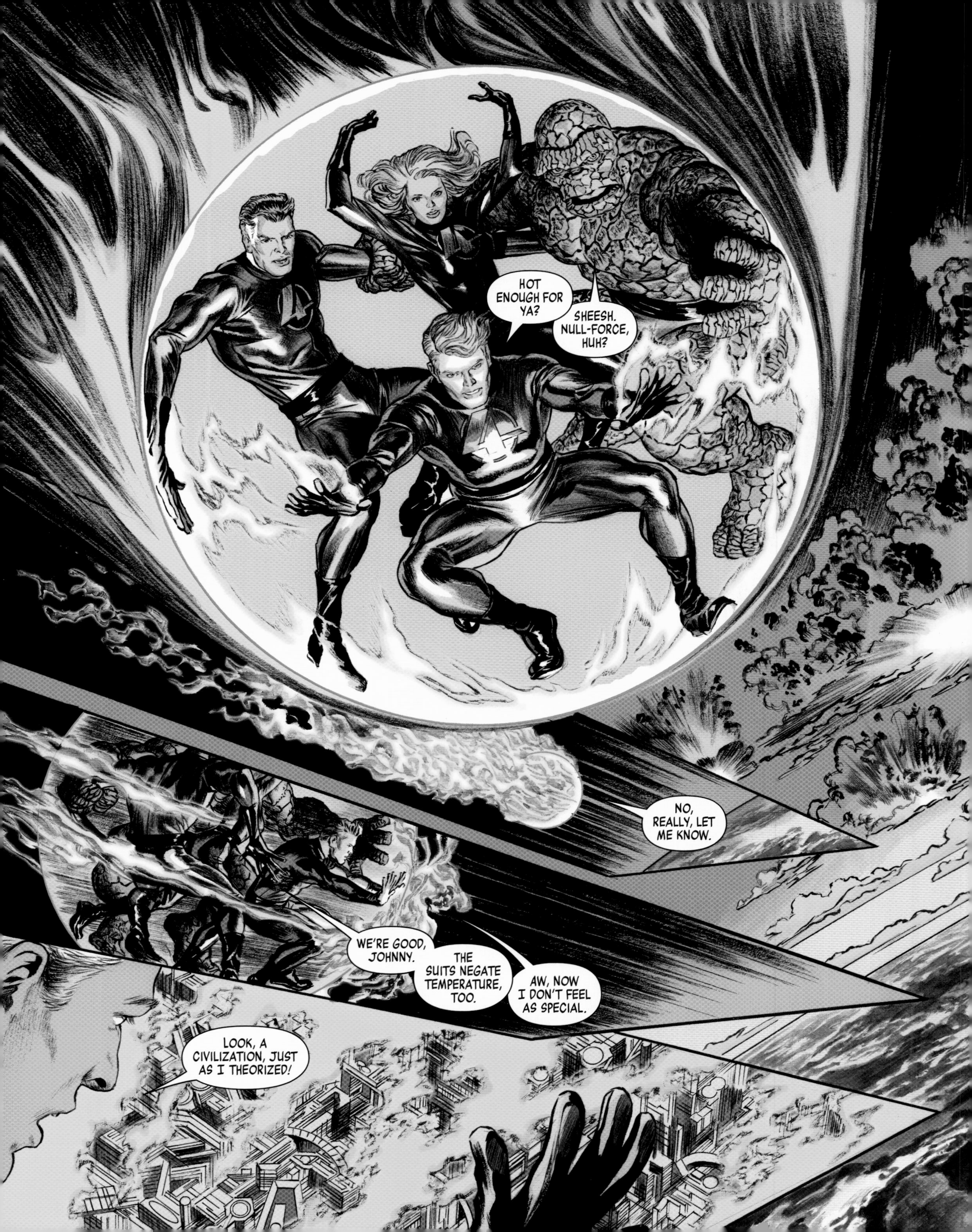
HOT ENOUGH FOR YA?
SHEESH. NULL-FORCE, HUH?
NO, REALLY, LET ME KNOW.
WE'RE GOOD, JOHNNY.
THE SUITS NEGATE TEMPERATURE, TOO.
AW, NOW I DON'T FEEL AS SPECIAL.
LOOK, A CIVILIZATION, JUST AS I THEORIZED!

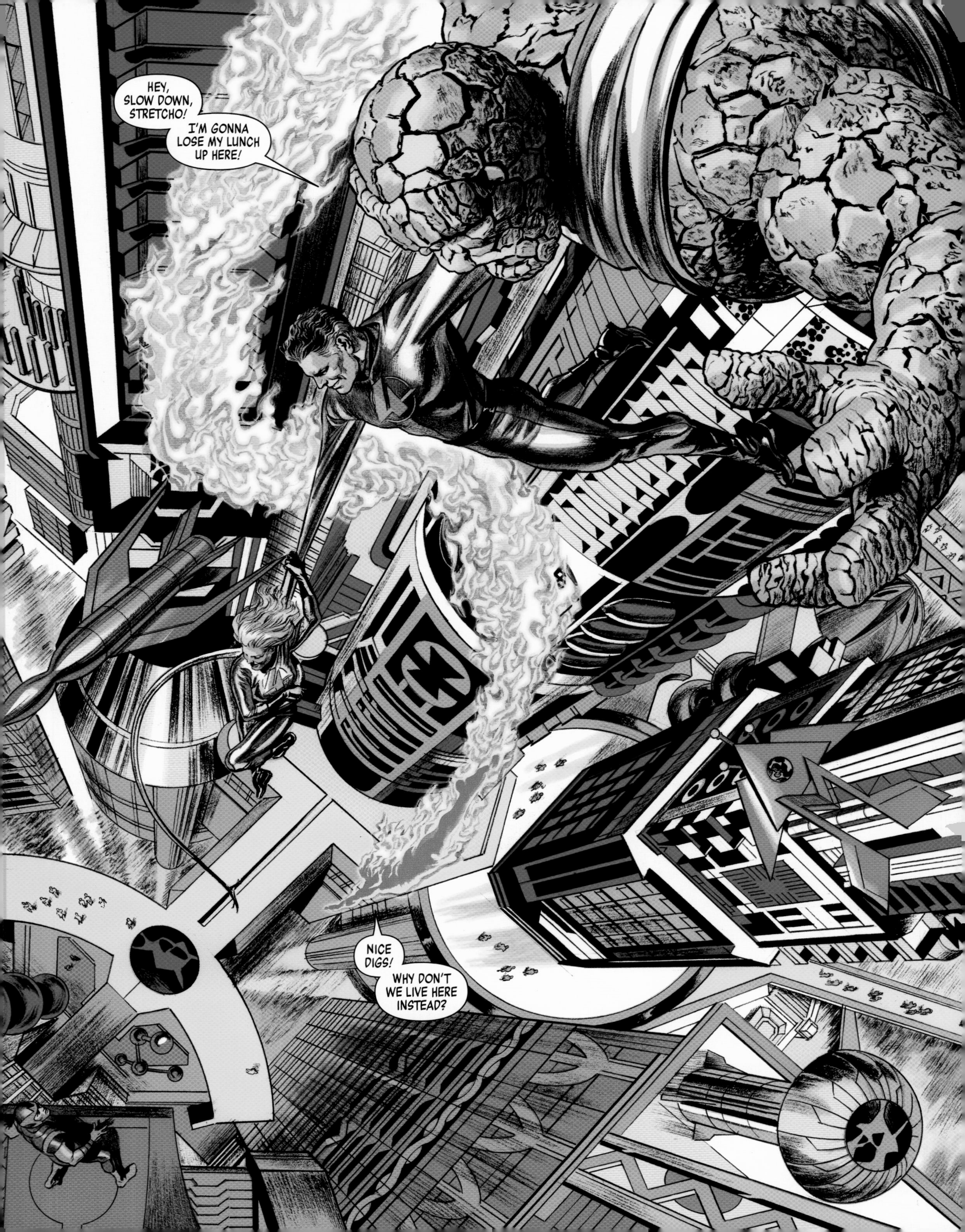
HEY, SLOW DOWN, STRETCHO!
I'M GONNA LOSE MY LUNCH UP HERE!
NICE DIGS!
WHY DON'T WE LIVE HERE INSTEAD?

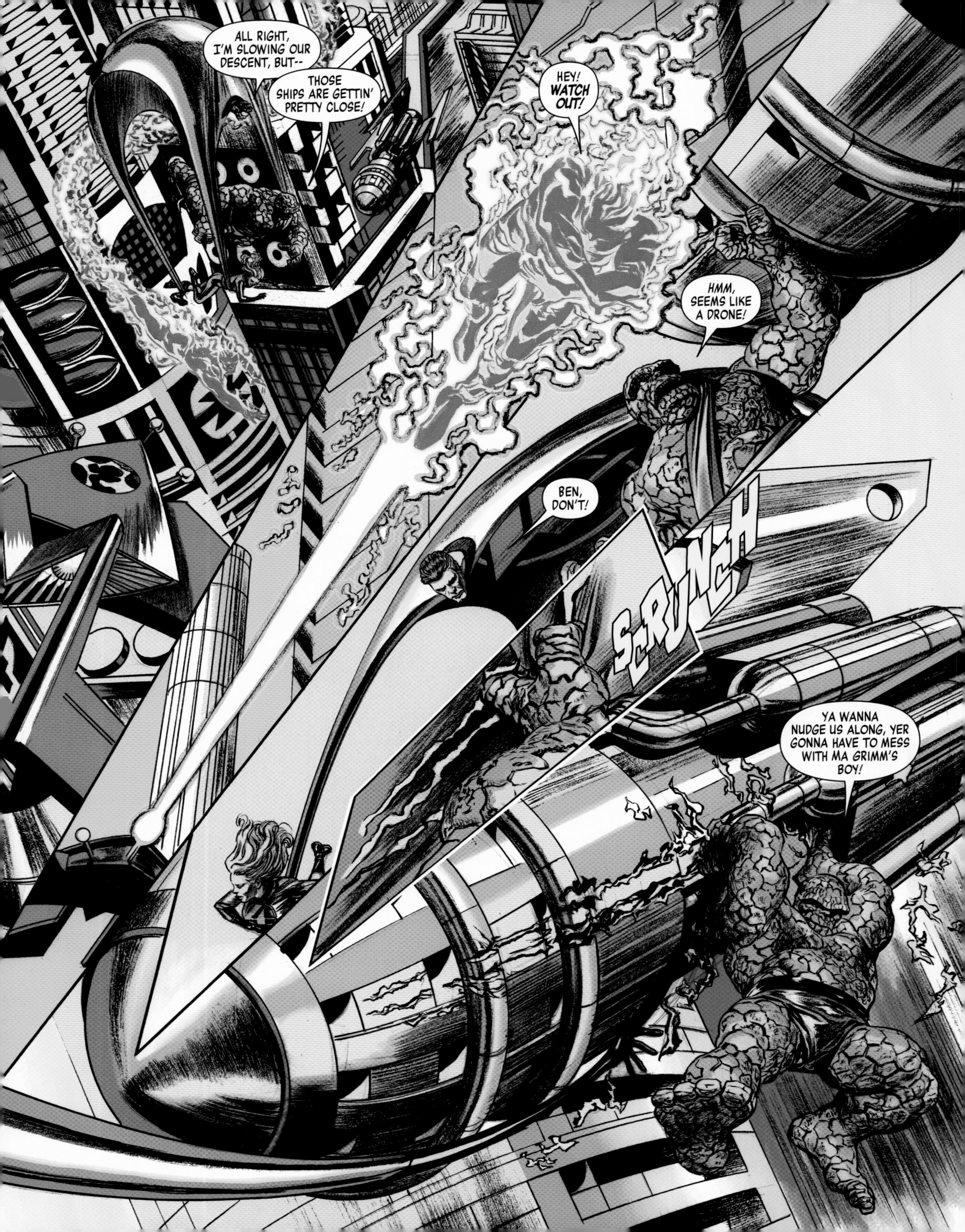
ALL RIGHT, I'M SLOWING OUR DESCENT, BUT--
THOSE SHIPS ARE GETTIN' PRETTY CLOSE!
HEY! WATCH OUT!
HMM, SEEMS LIKE A DRONE!
BEN, DON'T!
SCRUNCH
YA WANNA NUDGE US ALONG, YER GONNA HAVE TO MESS WITH MA GRIMM'S BOY!

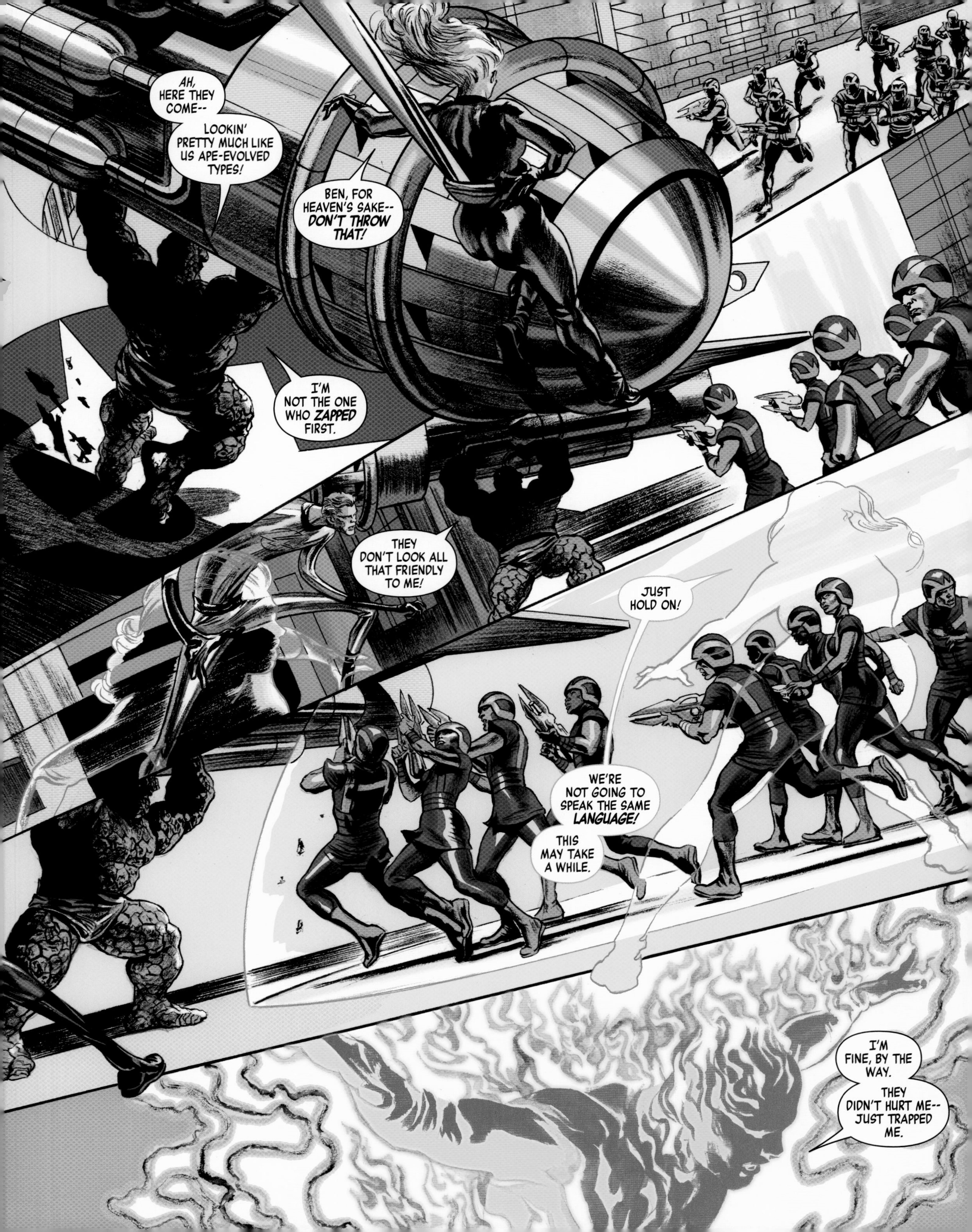
AH, HERE THEY COME--
LOOKIN' PRETTY MUCH LIKE US APE-EVOLVED TYPES!
BEN, FOR HEAVEN'S SAKE-- DON'T THROW THAT!
I'M NOT THE ONE WHO ZAPPED FIRST.
THEY DON'T LOOK ALL THAT FRIENDLY TO ME!
JUST HOLD ON!
WE'RE NOT GOING TO SPEAK THE SAME LANGUAGE!
THIS MAY TAKE A WHILE.
I'M FINE, BY THE WAY.
THEY DIDN'T HURT ME-- JUST TRAPPED ME.

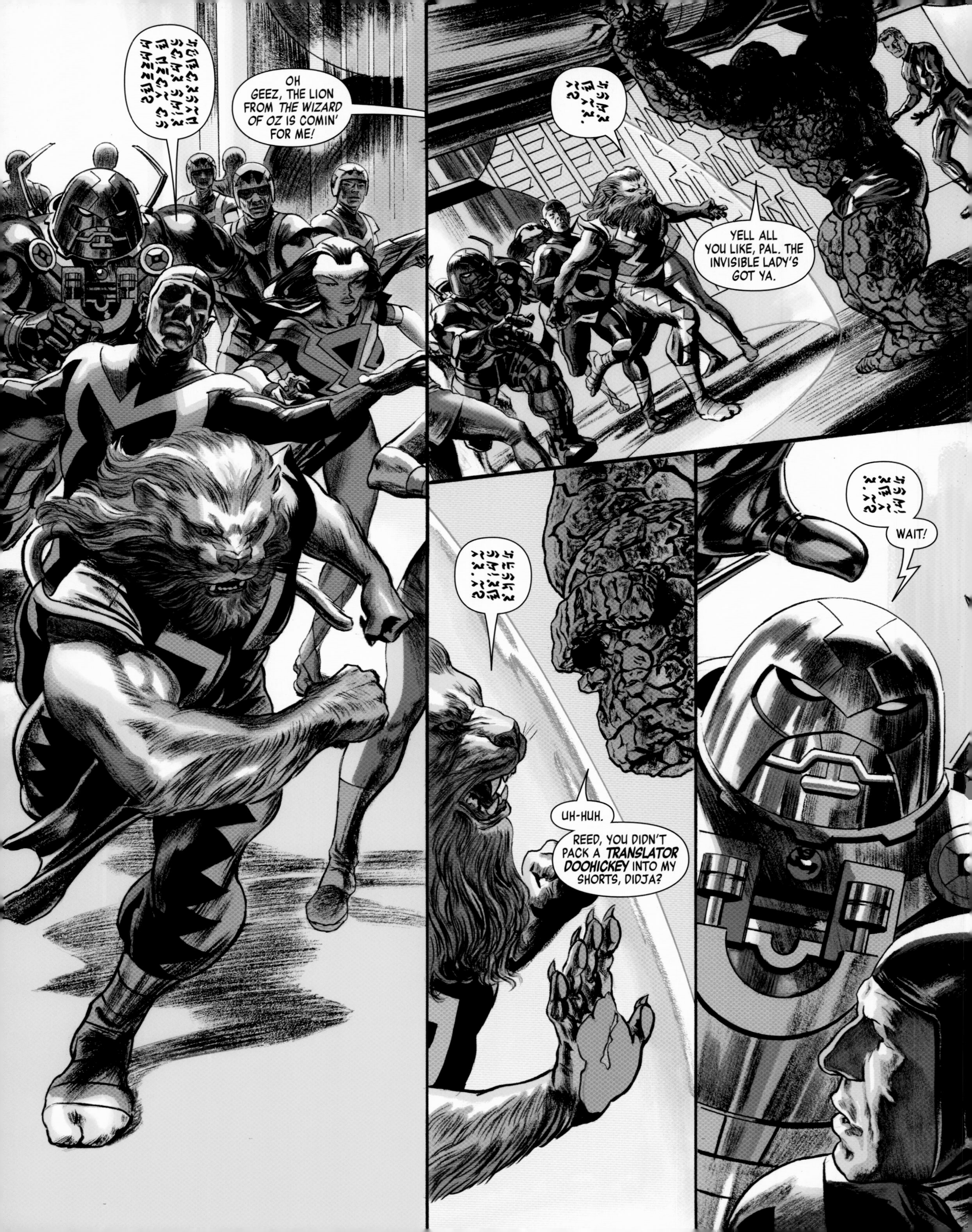
OH GEEZ, THE LION FROM *THE WIZARD OF OZ* IS COMIN' FOR ME!
YELL ALL YOU LIKE, PAL. THE INVISIBLE LADY'S GOT YA.
UH-HUH.
REED, YOU DIDN'T PACK A ***TRANSLATOR DOOHICKEY*** INTO MY SHORTS, DIDJA?
WAIT!

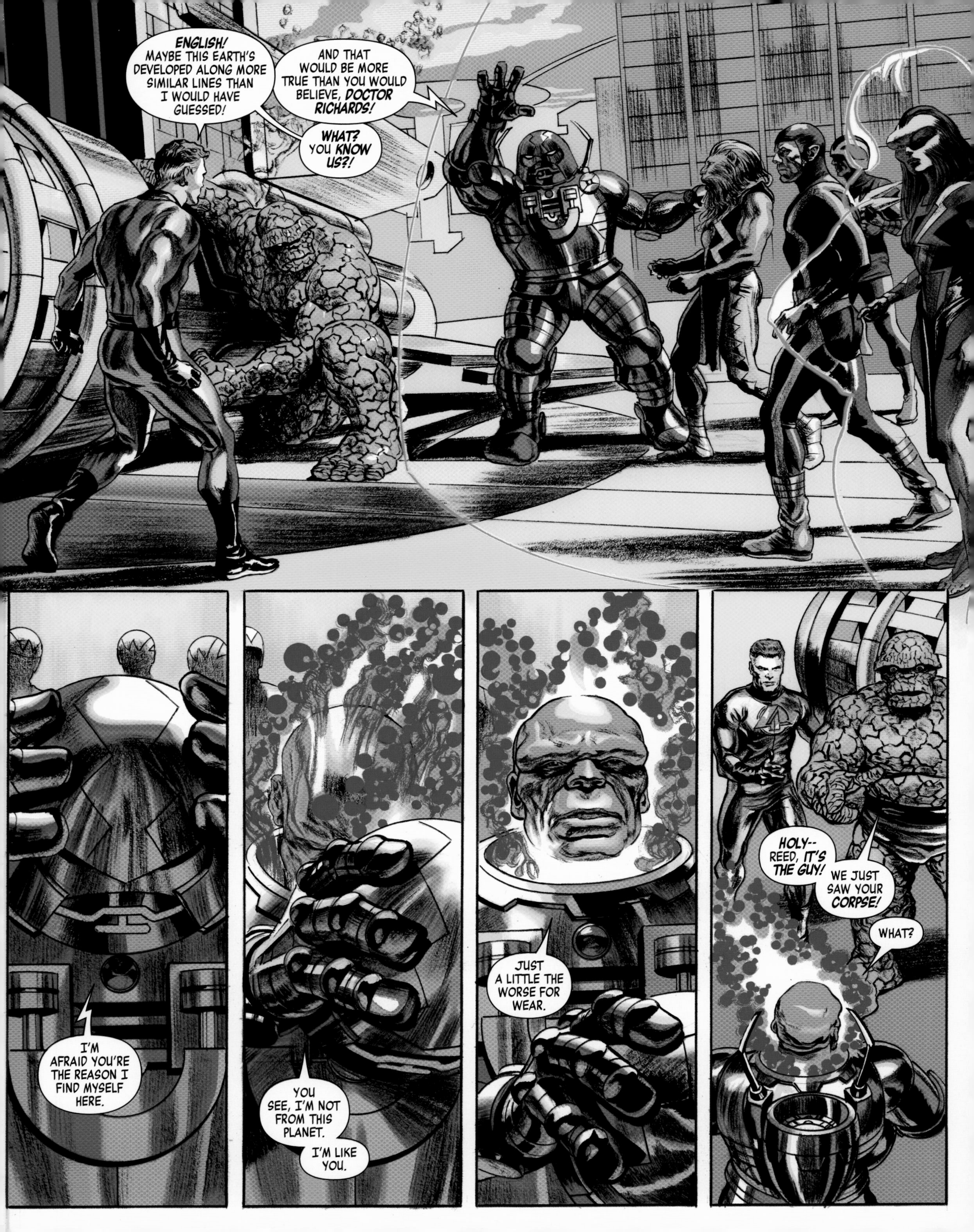
ENGLISH! MAYBE THIS EARTH'S DEVELOPED ALONG MORE SIMILAR LINES THAN I WOULD HAVE GUESSED!
AND THAT WOULD BE MORE TRUE THAN YOU WOULD BELIEVE, DOCTOR RICHARDS!
WHAT? YOU KNOW US?!
I'M AFRAID YOU'RE THE REASON I FIND MYSELF HERE.
YOU SEE, I'M NOT FROM THIS PLANET.
I'M LIKE YOU.
JUST A LITTLE THE WORSE FOR WEAR.
HOLY-- REED, IT'S THE GUY!
WE JUST SAW YOUR CORPSE!
WHAT?

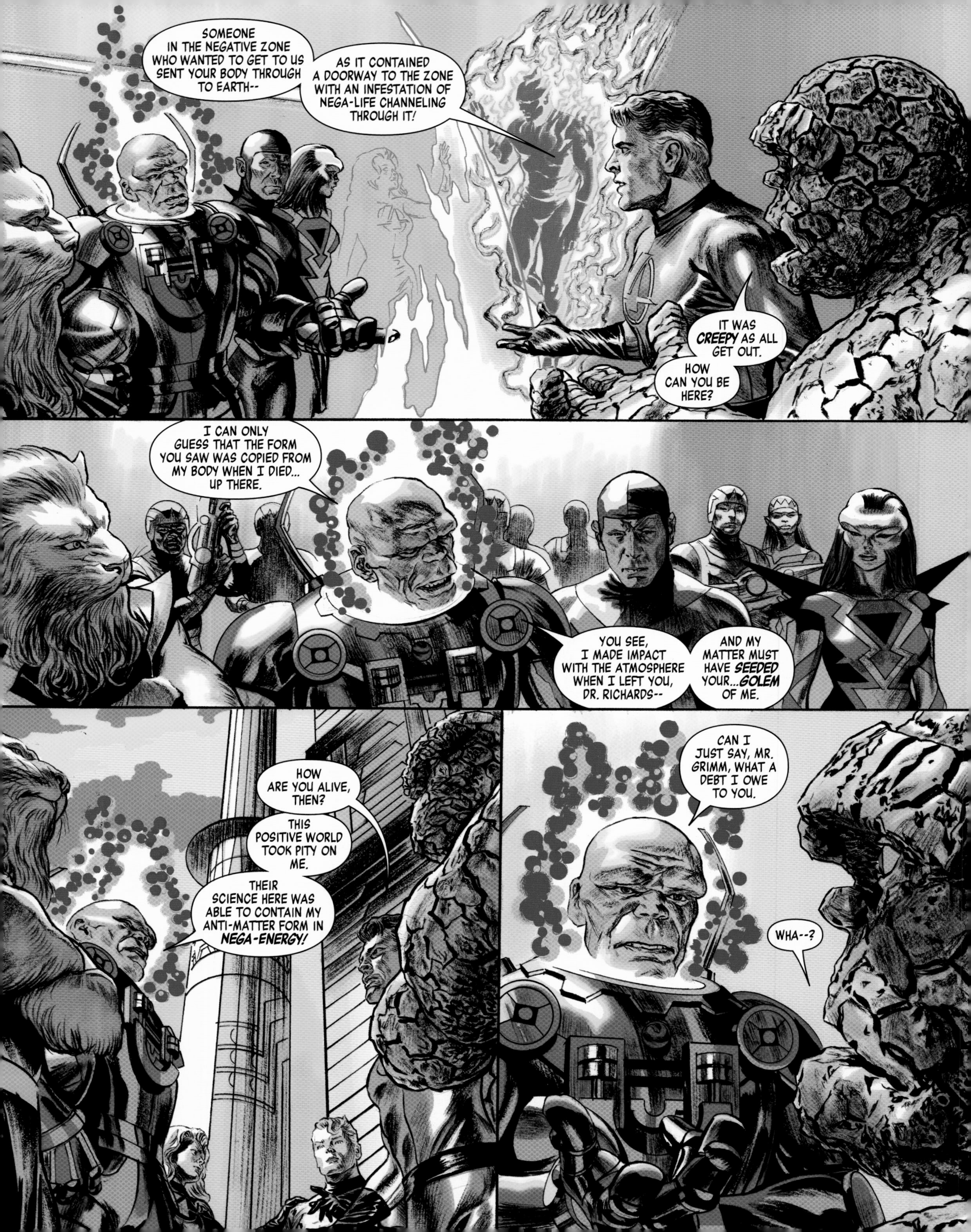
SOMEONE IN THE NEGATIVE ZONE WHO WANTED TO GET TO US SENT YOUR BODY THROUGH TO EARTH--
AS IT CONTAINED A DOORWAY TO THE ZONE WITH AN INFESTATION OF NEGA-LIFE CHANNELING THROUGH IT!
IT WAS CREEPY AS ALL GET OUT.
HOW CAN YOU BE HERE?
I CAN ONLY GUESS THAT THE FORM YOU SAW WAS COPIED FROM MY BODY WHEN I DIED... UP THERE.
YOU SEE, I MADE IMPACT WITH THE ATMOSPHERE WHEN I LEFT YOU, DR. RICHARDS--
AND MY MATTER MUST HAVE SEEDED YOUR...GOLEM OF ME.
HOW ARE YOU ALIVE, THEN?
THIS POSITIVE WORLD TOOK PITY ON ME.
THEIR SCIENCE HERE WAS ABLE TO CONTAIN MY ANTI-MATTER FORM IN NEGA-ENERGY!
CAN I JUST SAY, MR. GRIMM, WHAT A DEBT I OWE TO YOU.
WHA--?

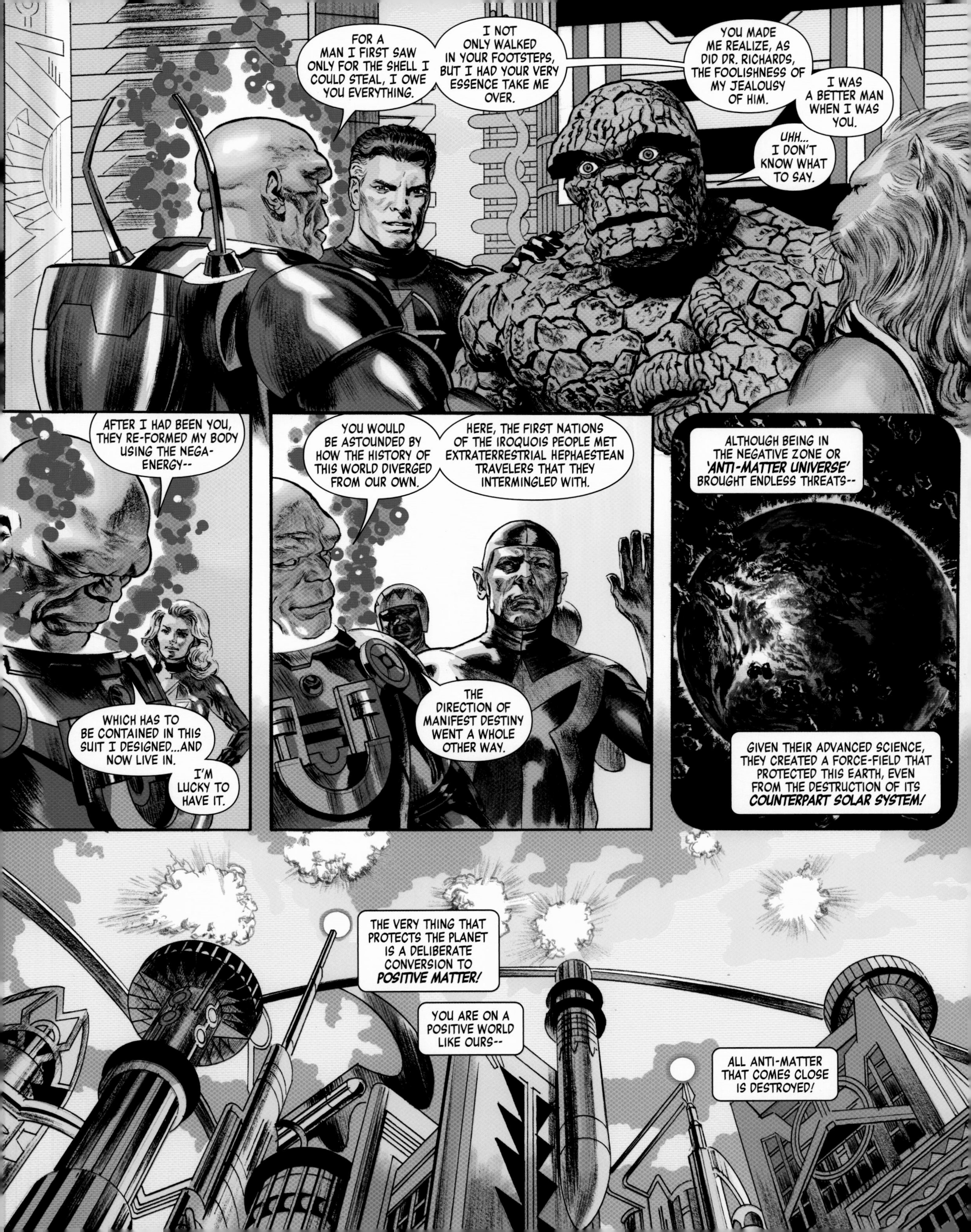
FOR A MAN I FIRST SAW ONLY FOR THE SHELL I COULD STEAL, I OWE YOU EVERYTHING.
I NOT ONLY WALKED IN YOUR FOOTSTEPS, BUT I HAD YOUR VERY ESSENCE TAKE ME OVER.
YOU MADE ME REALIZE, AS DID DR. RICHARDS, THE FOOLISHNESS OF MY JEALOUSY OF HIM.
I WAS A BETTER MAN WHEN I WAS YOU.
UHH... I DON'T KNOW WHAT TO SAY.
AFTER I HAD BEEN YOU, THEY RE-FORMED MY BODY USING THE NEGA-ENERGY--
WHICH HAS TO BE CONTAINED IN THIS SUIT I DESIGNED...AND NOW LIVE IN.
I'M LUCKY TO HAVE IT.
YOU WOULD BE ASTOUNDED BY HOW THE HISTORY OF THIS WORLD DIVERGED FROM OUR OWN.
HERE, THE FIRST NATIONS OF THE IROQUOIS PEOPLE MET EXTRATERRESTRIAL HEPHAESTEAN TRAVELERS THAT THEY INTERMINGLED WITH.
THE DIRECTION OF MANIFEST DESTINY WENT A WHOLE OTHER WAY.
ALTHOUGH BEING IN THE NEGATIVE ZONE OR *'ANTI-MATTER UNIVERSE'* BROUGHT ENDLESS THREATS--
GIVEN THEIR ADVANCED SCIENCE, THEY CREATED A FORCE-FIELD THAT PROTECTED THIS EARTH, EVEN FROM THE DESTRUCTION OF ITS ***COUNTERPART SOLAR SYSTEM!***
THE VERY THING THAT PROTECTS THE PLANET IS A DELIBERATE CONVERSION TO ***POSITIVE MATTER!***
YOU ARE ON A POSITIVE WORLD LIKE OURS--
ALL ANTI-MATTER THAT COMES CLOSE IS DESTROYED!

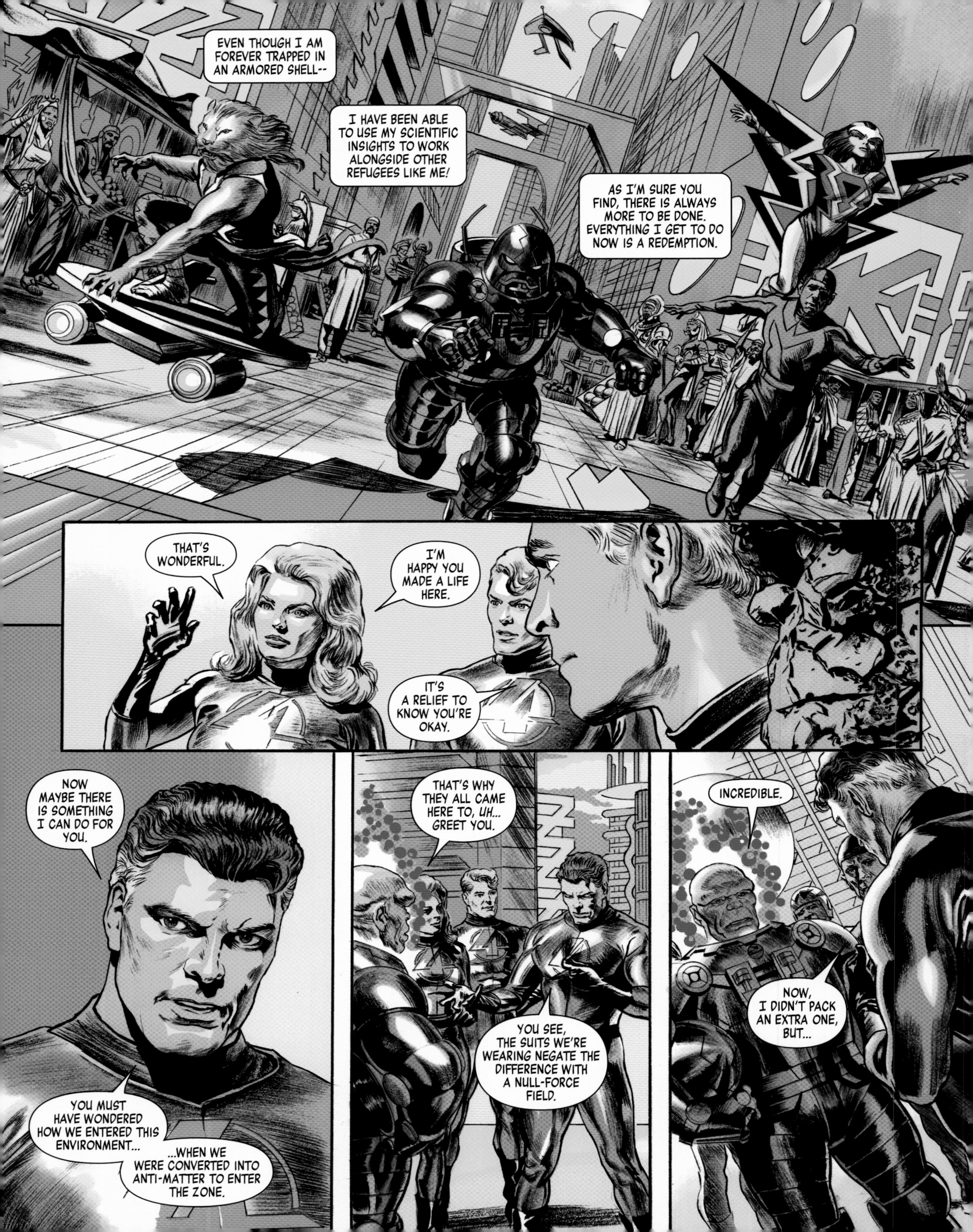
EVEN THOUGH I AM FOREVER TRAPPED IN AN ARMORED SHELL--
I HAVE BEEN ABLE TO USE MY SCIENTIFIC INSIGHTS TO WORK ALONGSIDE OTHER REFUGEES LIKE ME!
AS I'M SURE YOU FIND, THERE IS ALWAYS MORE TO BE DONE. EVERYTHING I GET TO DO NOW IS A REDEMPTION.
THAT'S WONDERFUL.
I'M HAPPY YOU MADE A LIFE HERE.
IT'S A RELIEF TO KNOW YOU'RE OKAY.
NOW MAYBE THERE IS SOMETHING I CAN DO FOR YOU.
YOU MUST HAVE WONDERED HOW WE ENTERED THIS ENVIRONMENT...
...WHEN WE WERE CONVERTED INTO ANTI-MATTER TO ENTER THE ZONE.
THAT'S WHY THEY ALL CAME HERE TO, UH... GREET YOU.
YOU SEE, THE SUITS WE'RE WEARING NEGATE THE DIFFERENCE WITH A NULL-FORCE FIELD.
INCREDIBLE.
NOW, I DIDN'T PACK AN EXTRA ONE, BUT...

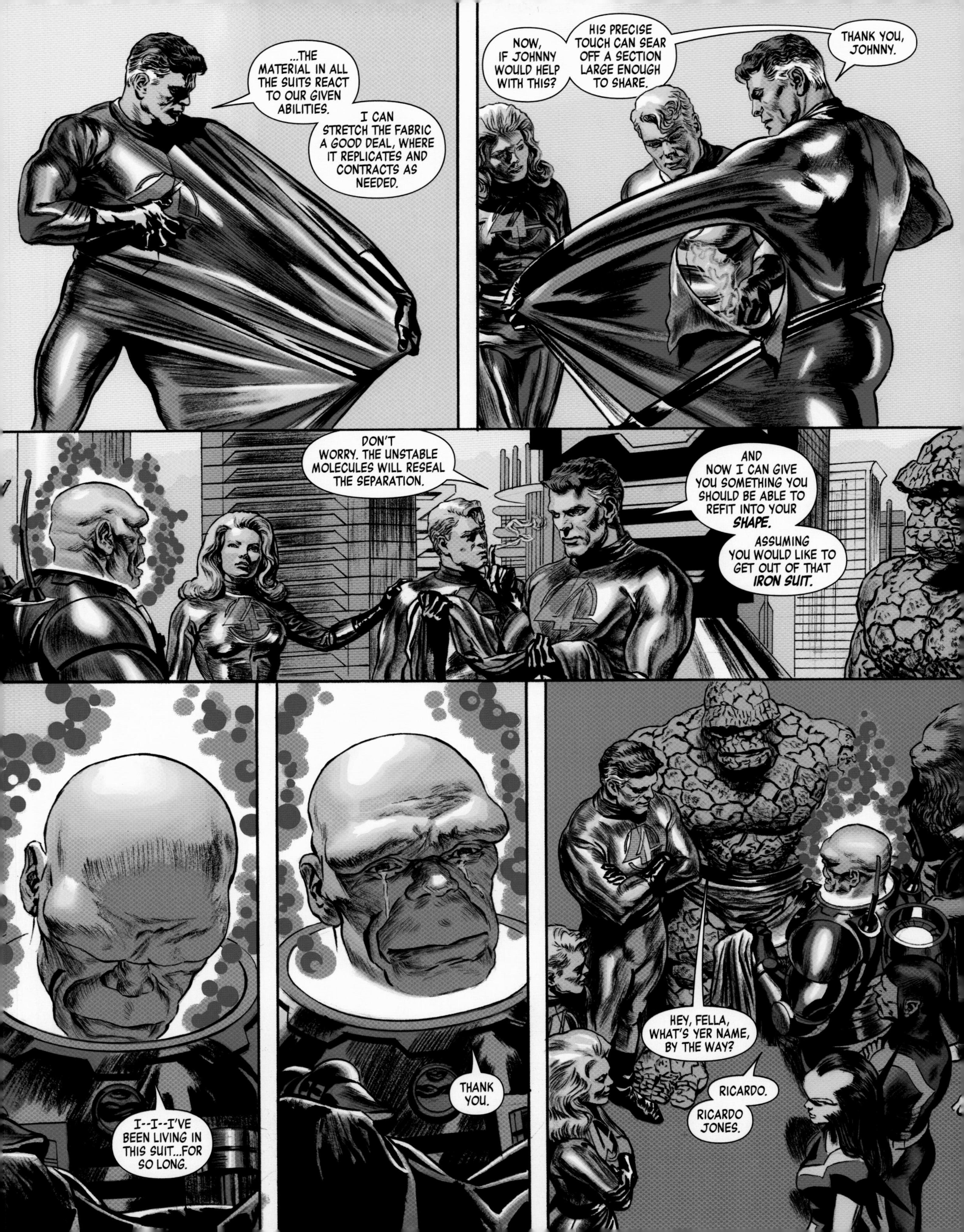
...THE MATERIAL IN ALL THE SUITS REACT TO OUR GIVEN ABILITIES.
I CAN STRETCH THE FABRIC A GOOD DEAL, WHERE IT REPLICATES AND CONTRACTS AS NEEDED.
NOW, IF JOHNNY WOULD HELP WITH THIS?
HIS PRECISE TOUCH CAN SEAR OFF A SECTION LARGE ENOUGH TO SHARE.
THANK YOU, JOHNNY.
DON'T WORRY. THE UNSTABLE MOLECULES WILL RESEAL THE SEPARATION.
AND NOW I CAN GIVE YOU SOMETHING YOU SHOULD BE ABLE TO REFIT INTO YOUR *SHAPE.*
ASSUMING YOU WOULD LIKE TO GET OUT OF THAT *IRON SUIT.*
I--I--I'VE BEEN LIVING IN THIS SUIT...FOR SO LONG.
THANK YOU.
HEY, FELLA, WHAT'S YER NAME, BY THE WAY?
RICARDO.
RICARDO JONES.

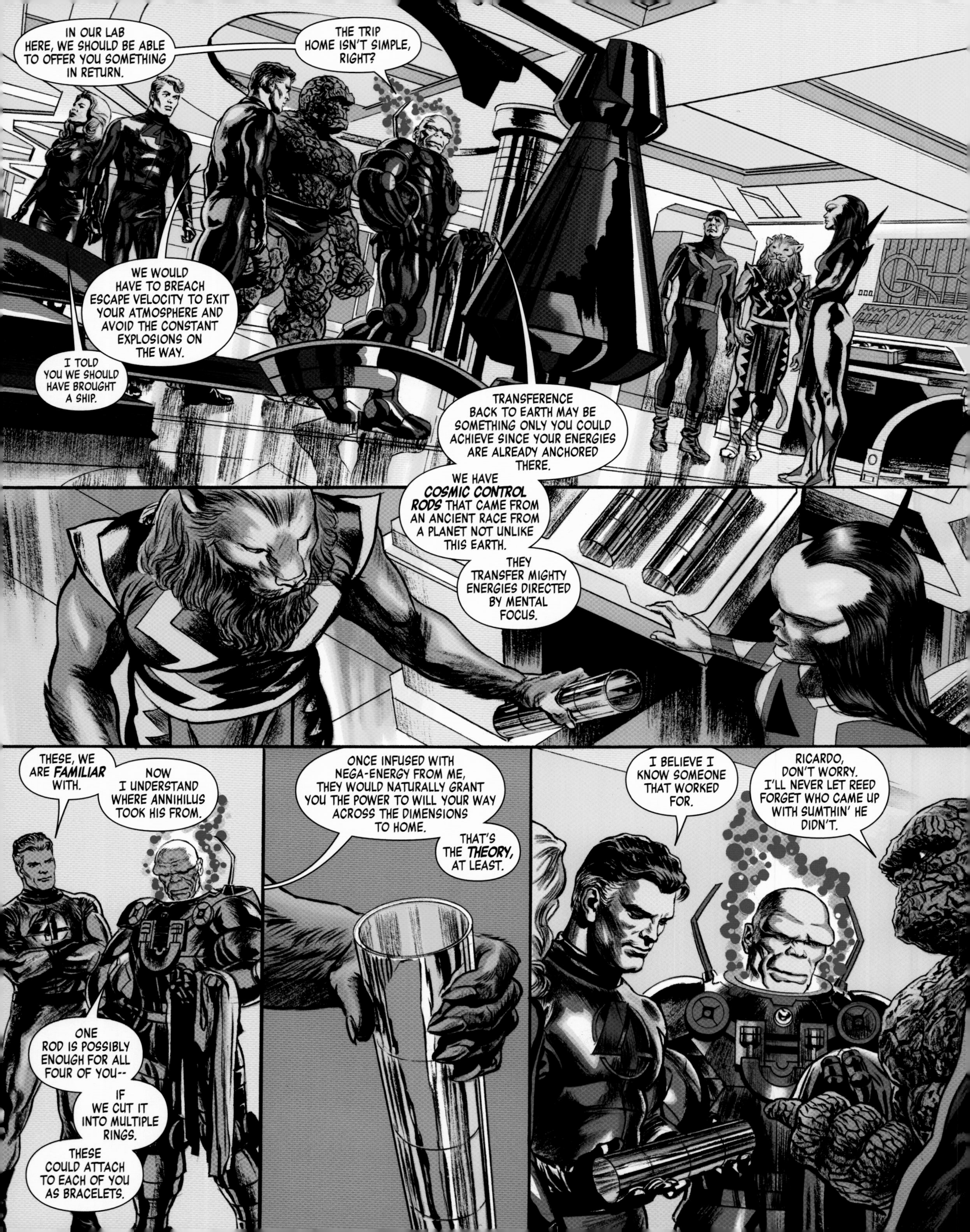
IN OUR LAB HERE, WE SHOULD BE ABLE TO OFFER YOU SOMETHING IN RETURN.
THE TRIP HOME ISN'T SIMPLE, RIGHT?
WE WOULD HAVE TO BREACH ESCAPE VELOCITY TO EXIT YOUR ATMOSPHERE AND AVOID THE CONSTANT EXPLOSIONS ON THE WAY.
I TOLD YOU WE SHOULD HAVE BROUGHT A SHIP.
TRANSFERENCE BACK TO EARTH MAY BE SOMETHING ONLY YOU COULD ACHIEVE SINCE YOUR ENERGIES ARE ALREADY ANCHORED THERE.
WE HAVE COSMIC CONTROL RODS THAT CAME FROM AN ANCIENT RACE FROM A PLANET NOT UNLIKE THIS EARTH.
THEY TRANSFER MIGHTY ENERGIES DIRECTED BY MENTAL FOCUS.
THESE, WE ARE FAMILIAR WITH.
NOW I UNDERSTAND WHERE ANNIHILUS TOOK HIS FROM.
ONE ROD IS POSSIBLY ENOUGH FOR ALL FOUR OF YOU--
IF WE CUT IT INTO MULTIPLE RINGS.
THESE COULD ATTACH TO EACH OF YOU AS BRACELETS.
ONCE INFUSED WITH NEGA-ENERGY FROM ME, THEY WOULD NATURALLY GRANT YOU THE POWER TO WILL YOUR WAY ACROSS THE DIMENSIONS TO HOME.
THAT'S THE THEORY, AT LEAST.
I BELIEVE I KNOW SOMEONE THAT WORKED FOR.
RICARDO, DON'T WORRY. I'LL NEVER LET REED FORGET WHO CAME UP WITH SUMTHIN' HE DIDN'T.

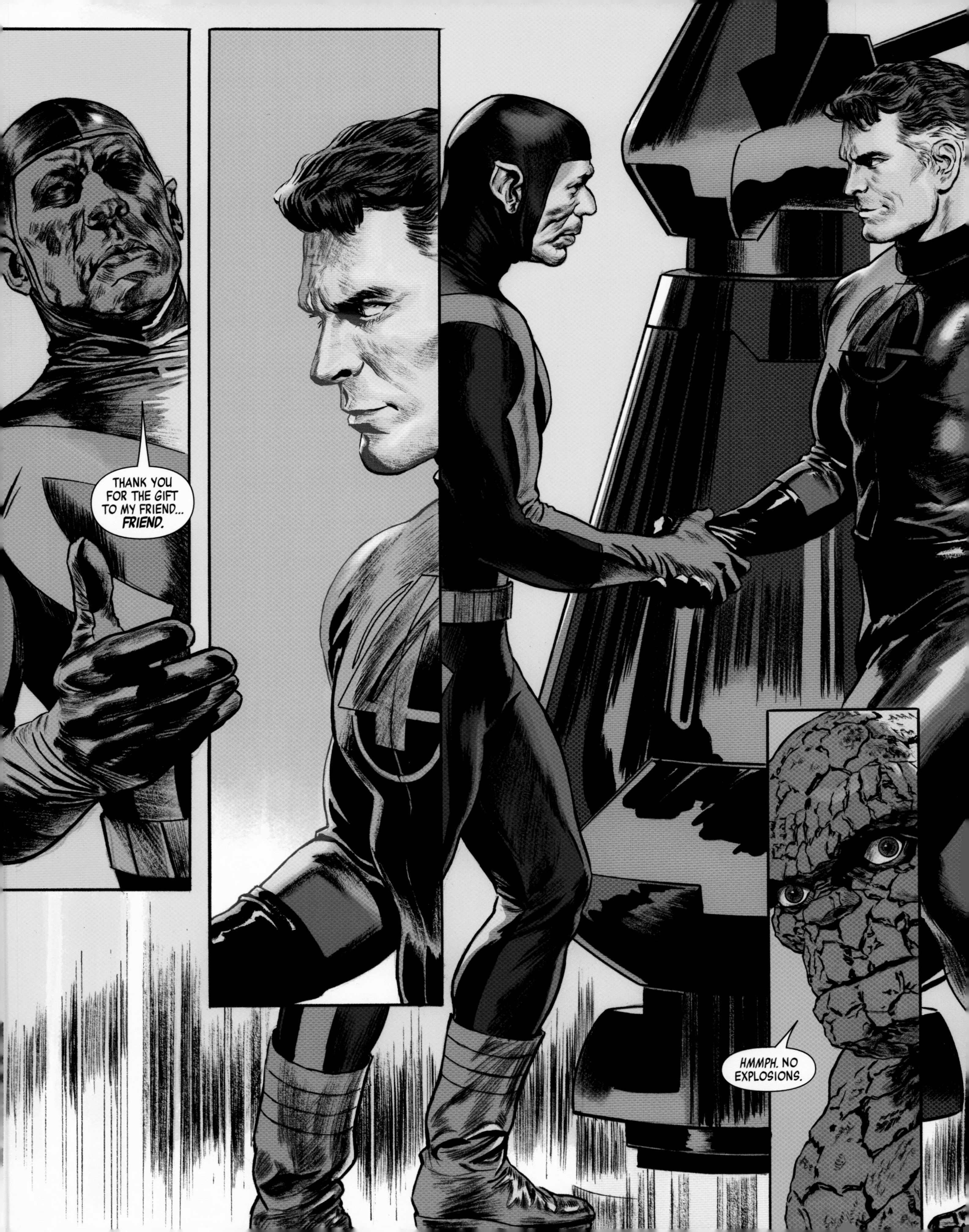
THANK YOU FOR THE GIFT TO MY FRIEND... FRIEND.
HMMPH. NO EXPLOSIONS.

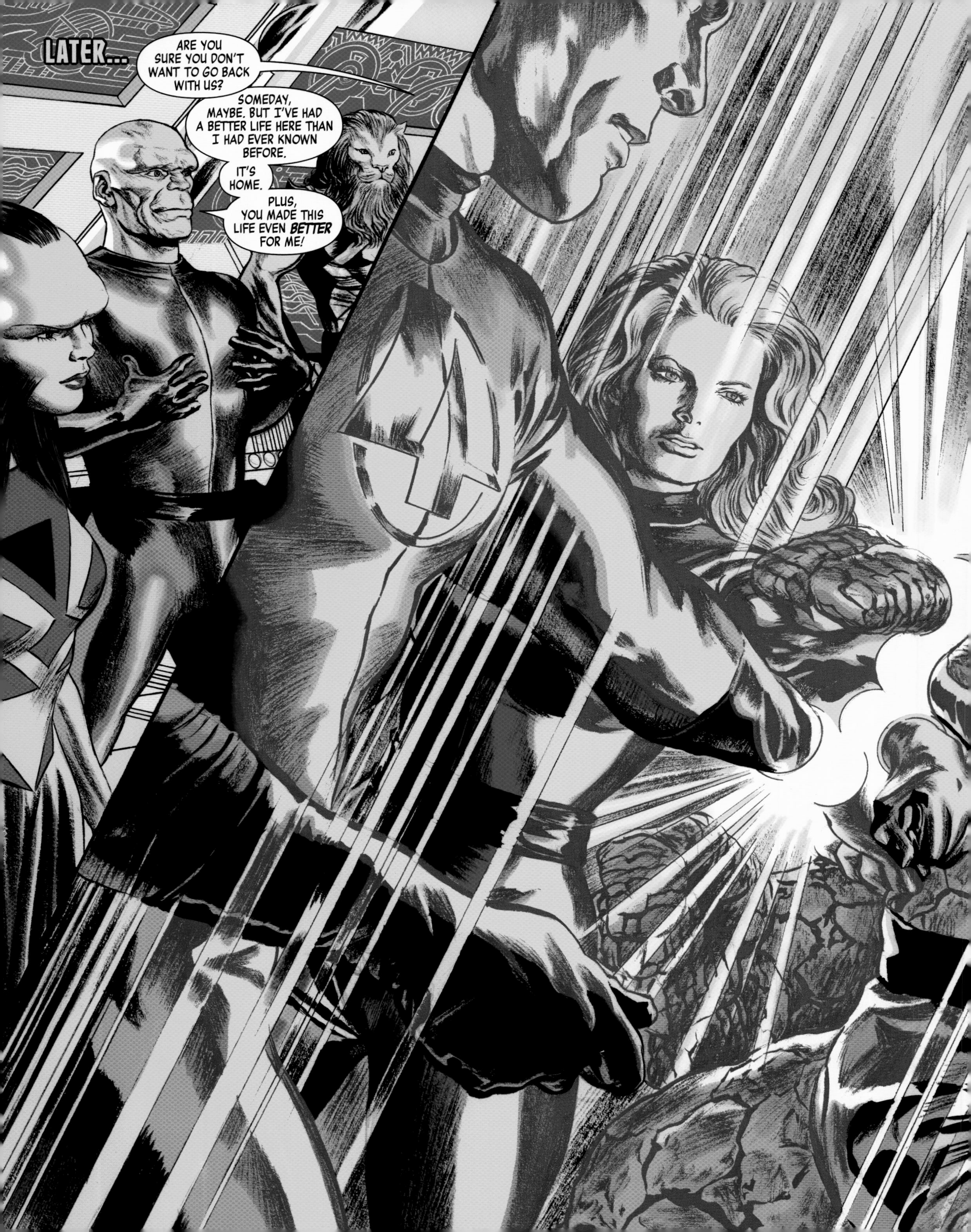
LATER...
ARE YOU SURE YOU DON'T WANT TO GO BACK WITH US?
SOMEDAY, MAYBE. BUT I'VE HAD A BETTER LIFE HERE THAN I HAD EVER KNOWN BEFORE.
IT'S HOME.
PLUS, YOU MADE THIS LIFE EVEN **BETTER** FOR ME!

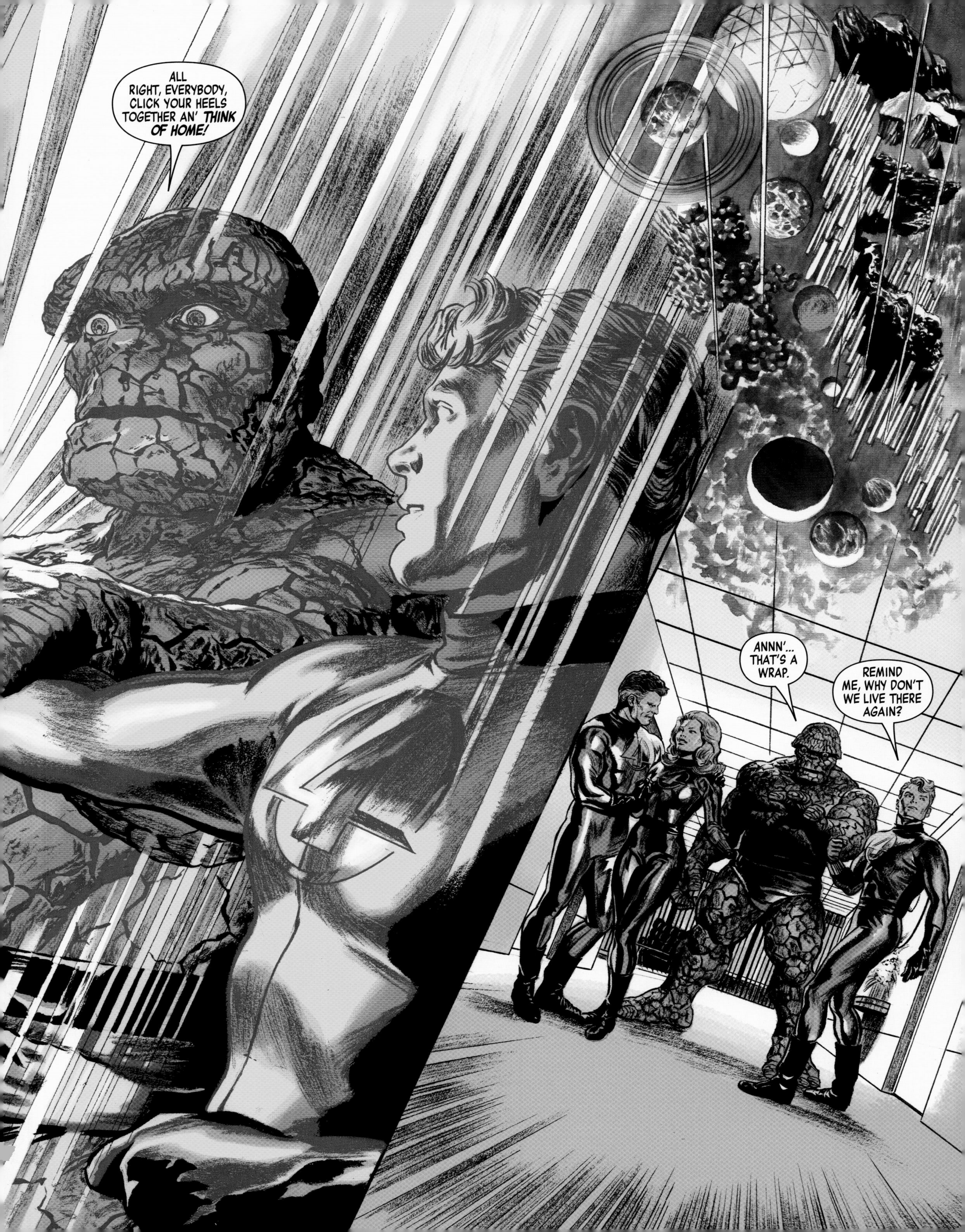
ALL RIGHT, EVERYBODY, CLICK YOUR HEELS TOGETHER AN' THINK OF HOME!
ANNN'... THAT'S A WRAP.
REMIND ME, WHY DON'T WE LIVE THERE AGAIN?

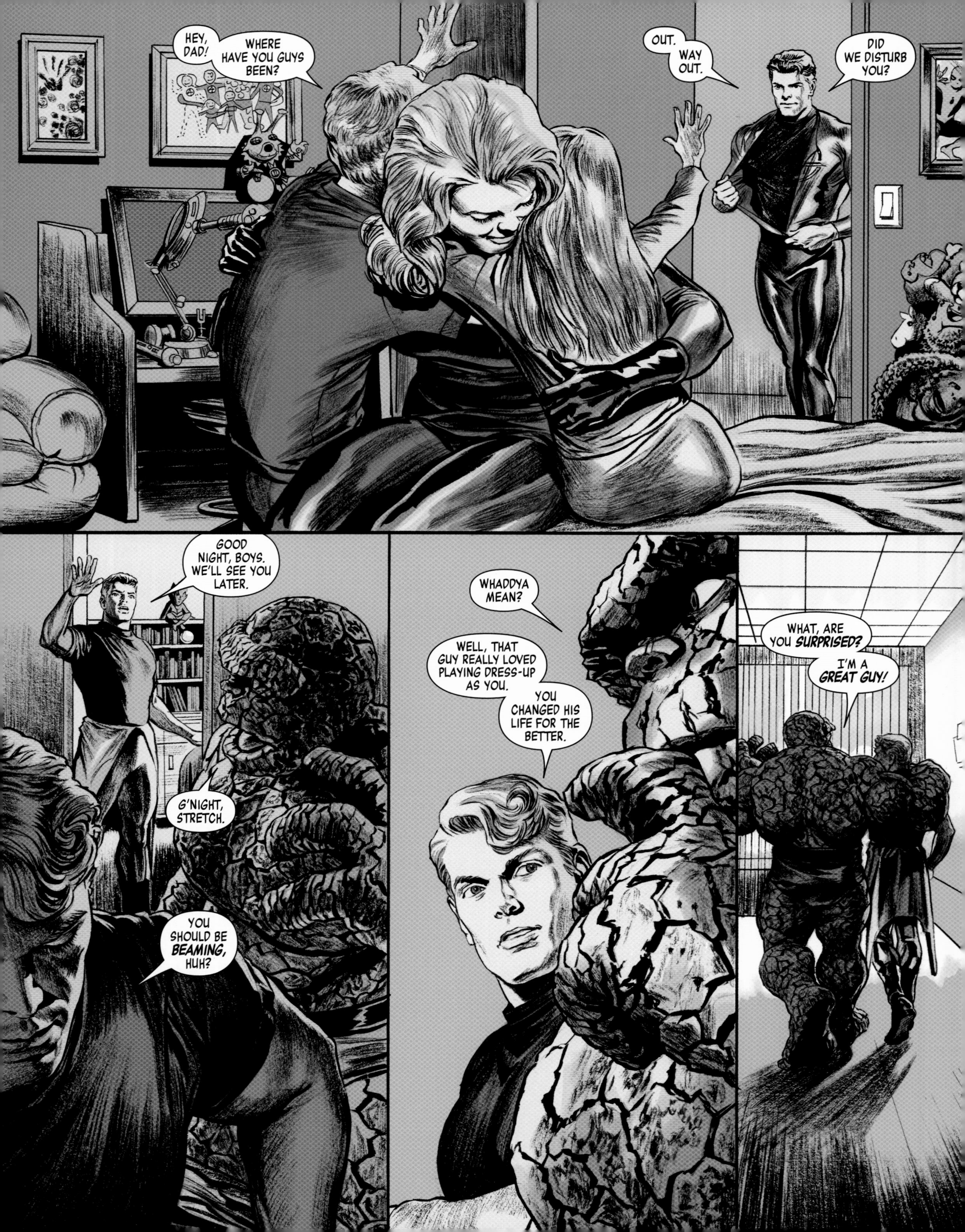
HEY, DAD!
WHERE HAVE YOU GUYS BEEN?
OUT. WAY OUT.
DID WE DISTURB YOU?
GOOD NIGHT, BOYS. WE'LL SEE YOU LATER.
G'NIGHT, STRETCH.
YOU SHOULD BE BEAMING, HUH?
WHADDYA MEAN?
WELL, THAT GUY REALLY LOVED PLAYING DRESS-UP AS YOU.
YOU CHANGED HIS LIFE FOR THE BETTER.
WHAT, ARE YOU SURPRISED?
I'M A GREAT GUY!

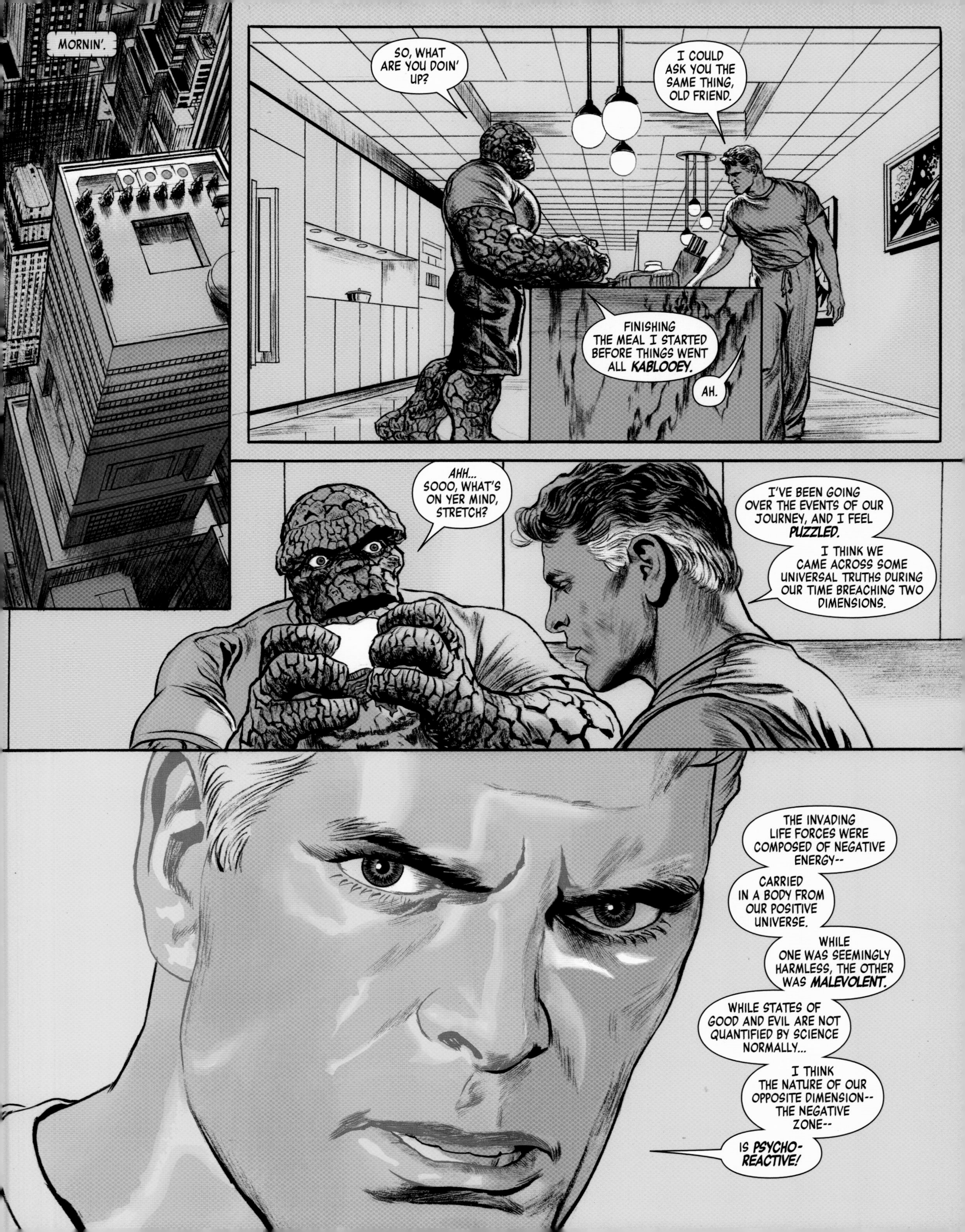
MORNIN'.
SO, WHAT ARE YOU DOIN' UP?
I COULD ASK YOU THE SAME THING, OLD FRIEND.
FINISHING THE MEAL I STARTED BEFORE THINGS WENT ALL **KABLOOEY.**
AH.
AHH... SOOO, WHAT'S ON YER MIND, STRETCH?
I'VE BEEN GOING OVER THE EVENTS OF OUR JOURNEY, AND I FEEL ***PUZZLED.***
I THINK WE CAME ACROSS SOME UNIVERSAL TRUTHS DURING OUR TIME BREACHING TWO DIMENSIONS.
THE INVADING LIFE FORCES WERE COMPOSED OF NEGATIVE ENERGY--
CARRIED IN A BODY FROM OUR POSITIVE UNIVERSE.
WHILE ONE WAS SEEMINGLY HARMLESS, THE OTHER WAS ***MALEVOLENT.***
WHILE STATES OF GOOD AND EVIL ARE NOT QUANTIFIED BY SCIENCE NORMALLY...
I THINK THE NATURE OF OUR OPPOSITE DIMENSION--THE NEGATIVE ZONE--
IS ***PSYCHO-REACTIVE!***

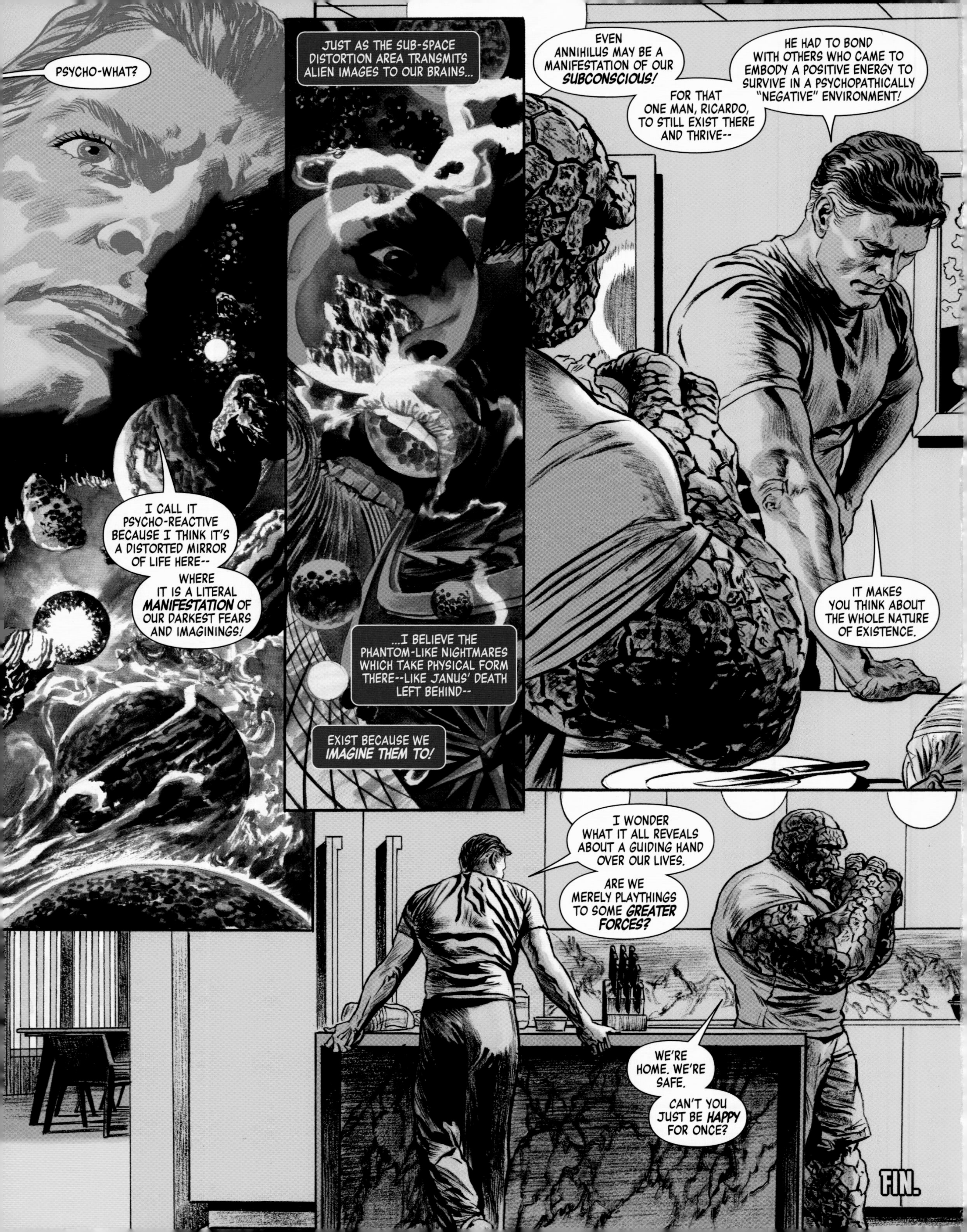
PSYCHO-WHAT?
JUST AS THE SUB-SPACE DISTORTION AREA TRANSMITS ALIEN IMAGES TO OUR BRAINS...
EVEN ANNIHILUS MAY BE A MANIFESTATION OF OUR SUBCONSCIOUS!
FOR THAT ONE MAN, RICARDO, TO STILL EXIST THERE AND THRIVE--
HE HAD TO BOND WITH OTHERS WHO CAME TO EMBODY A POSITIVE ENERGY TO SURVIVE IN A PSYCHOPATHICALLY "NEGATIVE" ENVIRONMENT!
I CALL IT PSYCHO-REACTIVE BECAUSE I THINK IT'S A DISTORTED MIRROR OF LIFE HERE--
WHERE IT IS A LITERAL MANIFESTATION OF OUR DARKEST FEARS AND IMAGININGS!
...I BELIEVE THE PHANTOM-LIKE NIGHTMARES WHICH TAKE PHYSICAL FORM THERE--LIKE JANUS' DEATH LEFT BEHIND--
EXIST BECAUSE WE IMAGINE THEM TO!
IT MAKES YOU THINK ABOUT THE WHOLE NATURE OF EXISTENCE.
I WONDER WHAT IT ALL REVEALS ABOUT A GUIDING HAND OVER OUR LIVES.
ARE WE MERELY PLAYTHINGS TO SOME GREATER FORCES?
WE'RE HOME. WE'RE SAFE.
CAN'T YOU JUST BE HAPPY FOR ONCE?
FIN.

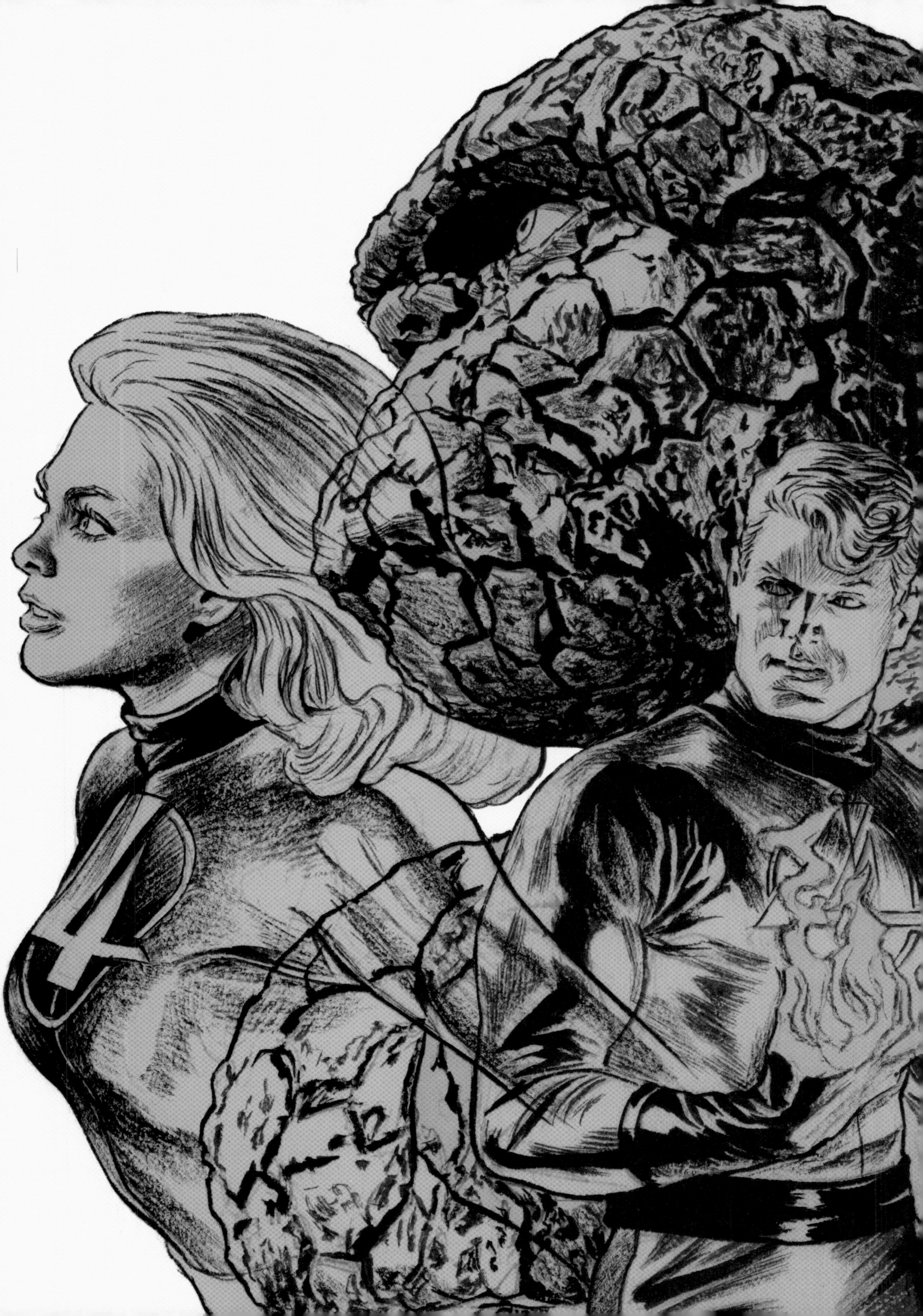